The Golden Sayings Of The Blessed Brother Giles Of Assisi

Paschal Robinson

Alpha Editions

This Edition Published in 2021

ISBN: 9789354413391

Design and Setting By
Alpha Editions
www.alphaedis.com
Email – info@alphaedis.com

As per information held with us this book is in Public Domain.
This book is a reproduction of an important historical work. Alpha Editions uses the best technology to reproduce historical work in the same manner it was first published to preserve its original nature. Any marks or number seen are left intentionally to preserve its true form.

TO

HIS EXCELLENCY

Mgr. Diomede Falconio

ARCHBISHOP OF LARISSA

APOSTOLIC DELEGATE

CONTENTS

INTRODUCTION

	Page
I. Blessed Giles: An Outline of his Life	vii
II. His Golden Sayings	xlvi
Origin	xlvii
Characteristics	xlviii
Early MS. Collections	li
Editions and Translations	lv

THE GOLDEN SAYINGS

Prologue	3
I. On Virtues and Graces and their Effects and Contrariwise of Vices	4
II. On Faith and the Incomprehensibility of God	6
III. On Love	9
IV. On Holy Humility	12
V. On the Holy Fear of the Lord	15
VI. On Patience	17
VII. On Holy Solicitude and Watchfulness of Heart	23
VIII. On Contempt of the World	28
IX. On Holy Chastity	30
X. On the Combat with Temptations	34
XI. On Penance	39
XII. On Prayer and its Effect	40
XIII. On Contemplation	46
XIV. On the Active Life	49

Contents

		Page
XV.	On the Continual Exercise of Spiritual Caution	51
XVI.	On Useful and Useless Knowledge and on Preachers of the Word of God	53
XVII.	On Words that are Good and not Good	56
XVIII.	On Perseverance in Good	58
XIX.	On Religion and the Safety Thereof	60
XX.	On Obedience and its Utility	64
XXI.	On the Recollection of Death	67
XXII.	On Shunning the World	68
XXIII.	On Perseverance in Prayer	69
XXIV.	On the Graces and Virtues which are acquired in Prayer	71
XXV.	On the Negligence of Prelates in the Canonization of Certain Friars	74
XXVI.	How Blessed Giles settled Sundry Noteworthy Questions	76

APPENDIX I

I.	On the Fear of God	81
II.	On those who are in Favor and Disfavor with God	86
III.	Admonitions on Preaching and Working	91
IV.	On Good Works and Correspondence with Grace	93
V.	On Gratitude and Contrition	97
VI.	Three Notable Sayings from the Book of Conformities	106

APPENDIX II

Some Additional Sayings from the Assisi MSS. Nos. 403 and 676 107

BIBLIOGRAPHY 121

GENERAL INDEX 131

ILLUSTRATIONS

Blessed Giles . . . . *Frontispiece*
    From the Medallion by Benozzo Gozzoli at
    S. Francesco, Montefalco

Meeting of Blessed Giles with St. Louis . . *Page* xlv
    After a fourteenth century panel in the
    Pinacoteca at Perugia

Hermitage of S. Maria Delle Carceri . . .   " lvi
    View from the opposite side of the ravine

Grotto of Blessed Giles at the Carceri . *Facing page* 8
    From a photograph specially taken for
    this volume

Convent at Monteripido . . . .   "   40
    Looking from Perugia

Cathedral of S. Lorenzo, Perugia . . . . . "   112
    From a photograph by Anderson, Rome

"Beatus autem Franciscus videns fratrem Ægidium gratia et virtute perfectum et paratum ac promptum ad omne opus bonum, intime diligebat eum et de ipso aliis fratribus aliquando dicebat: 'Iste est miles meus tabulæ rotundæ.'"—"Chronica XXIV Generalium," in *Anal. Francis.*, iii, p. 78.

INTRODUCTION

THERE existed in the Franciscan Order from an early date a school of asceticism, remarkable no less for great elevation of thought than for singular vivacity and picturesqueness of expression. This two-fold characteristic is perhaps nowhere more happily blended than in the *Dicta Aurea* of Blessed Giles of Assisi, a work which the Bollandists do not hesitate to rank at the head of its class [1] and which is here presented to the reader in an English dress.

No one at all conversant with things Franciscan need be told that Blessed Giles was of that stalwart little band who "were with the Blessed Francis from the time he began to have companions." "The Knight of our Round Table," St. Francis called him, and Giles remains the ideal type of the Franciscan Friar. It may not then be amiss to preface our study of his "Golden Sayings" with some account, however brief, of the long, strange life and the surroundings of their author.

[1] See "Analecta Bollandiana," t. xxiv (1905), p. 410.

Nearly a century ago the great Conventual critic Papini sighed for an adequate biography of Blessed Giles.[2] Some eight years since, a learned member of the same Order essayed to produce one,[3] but his volume falls short of the mark;[4] and the same is true of Mgr. Briganti's monograph published about the same time.[5] Neither of these books should be read with too critical an eye. On the other hand, the recent work of Father Gisbert Menge[6] — a seasoned scholar in all that concerns the subject — goes far toward meeting all modern requirements. But the finally acceptable biography of Giles

[2] "Il voto del Pubblico," he says, "e specialmente delle Città di Perugia e d'Assisi sarebbe d'averne la vita stampata, completa e sincera. Chi sa, che un giorno non spunti penna felice ad appagare le communi brame, giacchè di farlo non è ora a me dato." — "La Storia di S. Francesco," Foligno, 1827, l. ii, p. 212.

[3] P. Giuseppe Fratini, M. Conv.: "Vita del B. Egidio d'Assisi" (Assisi, Tip. Metastasio, 1898) in 16, pp. xvi-144.

[4] As Fr. Van Ortroy, S. J., remarks: "Ce travail nous parait prématuré. Il aurait fallu d'abord consulter les biographies encores inédites du bienheureux et surtout passer toute cette littérature au crible de la critique." — "Anal. Bolland.," t. xvii (1898), p. 380. See also "Miscellanea Francescana," vol. vi, fasc. 1 (1898), p. 30.

[5] Mons. Antonio Briganti: "Il Beato Egidio d'Assisi." Monografia. (Napoli, M. d'Auria, 1898), in 16, pp. xii-356; on this work see "Anal. Bolland.," t. xix, p. 72, and "Miscell. Frances.," vol. vii, fasc. iv (1899), p. 137.

[6] "Der Selige Aegidius von Assisi," Sein Leben und seine Sprüche. Von P. Gisbert Menge, O.F.M. Paderborn, Junfermann, 1906, in 12, pp. xvi-118. See "Theologisch-praktische Quartalschrift" (Linz), 1906, III Heft, pp. 609-610.

still remains to be written. Happily, however, we are able to go behind Giles's more recent biographers to some of the early documents from which our knowledge of him is derived.

Now Giles's first historian was none other than his life-long friend Brother Leo, the secretary and confessor of St. Francis. On this point we have the explicit testimony of Salimbene [7] who lived contemporaneously with both. Unfortunately, however, most of the writings of *Fra Pecorello di Dio* disappeared or rather lost their identity before the middle of the fourteenth century. That century, as I have elsewhere pointed out,[8] was for Franciscan history a *saeculum compilationis,* and Leo's life of Giles passed along with the rest into several of the compilations of *materia seraphica* which were then the order of the day. That it suffered as a consequence many excisions and not a little working over is clear from the incomplete and often altered versions of this Leonine life which have come down to us.

The well-known "Chronica XXIV Generalium," a compilation of about the middle of

[7] He writes:—" Fuit autem Fr. Aegidius qui Perusii in arca saxea tumulatus est in ecclesia Fratrum Minorum . . . cujus vita Fr. Leo, qui fuit unus (Rufinus et Angelus erant alii) de tribus specialibus sociis beati Francisci, sufficienter descripsit." See Salimbene, O.F.M., "Chronicon." (Ed. Parm. 1857), p. 323.

[8] See "Some Pages of Franciscan History," C.T.S., London, 1906.

the fourteenth century, but containing many early documents,[9] includes under the title of "Vita Fratris Aegidii viri sanctissimi et contemplativi"[10] a biography which Papini,[11] among others, regarded as the genuine handiwork of Leo, but which M. Paul Sabatier[12] and modern critics generally consider a mutilated and interpolated abridgment of the original document.

In 1901 Father Leonard Lemmens published another "Vita Fratris Aegidii," based on a fourteenth century codex at St. Isidore's College, Rome;[13] but his claim that this short life,

---

[9] This Chronicle, which was completed in 1379, is attributed to Fr. Arnold of Sarano, Provincial of Aquitaine. It has been published in the "Analecta Franciscana," t. iii (1897), by the Friars Minor at Quaracchi.

[10] See "Chron. XXIV General.," l. c., pp. 74-115.

[11] See Papini: "Notizie sicure," etc., 2 edit. (Foligno, 1824), p. 126.

[12] M. Sabatier writes: "Le compilateur de la Chronique des XXIV Généreaux qui nous l'a conservée lui a infligé le même traitement qu'à ses autres sources. Voulant abréger il n' a conservé que les faits qui lui paraissaient les plus intéressants, les récits merveilleux et il a supprimé entre eux les parties narratives. On voit les écueils d'une pareille méthode. Il voulait nous donner l'essence d'une legende et il nous a gardé qu'un catalogue." See "Speculum Perfectionis," ed. Sabatier, Paris, 1898, p. xcvi. Fr. Van Ortroy, S.J. ("Anal. Bolland.," t. xix, p. 135), and Fr. Leonard Lemmens, O.F.M. ("Doc. Antiqua Franciscana," pars i, p. 13) are of like opinion.

[13] Codex 1/63. See "Scripta Fratris Leonis" in "Documenta Antiqua Franciscana," pars i (Quaracchi, 1901), pp. 37-63, and pars iii, pp. 6-12.

which is different from that inserted in the "Chronica XXIV Generalium" and much less developed, represented the original Leonine life in its integrity, has not been admitted by critics in general. It is regarded by Fr. Van Ortroy[14] and others as an abridgment of a larger work from which the more ample biography in the "Chronica XXIV Generalium" may be derived through another channel.

Be this as it may, it seems certain that the "Historia Vitæ B. Aegidii," edited by the Bollandists[15] after a MS. formerly preserved in the sacristy of the Franciscan Convent at Perugia, but now lost, represents a still greater falling away from the text of Brother Leo.[16]

It remains to be seen whether or not the "Vita Beati Fratris Aegidii Assisiensis auctore Fratre Leone," promised by M. Sabatier for publication in the "Collection d'Etudes," may tend to make for the rehabilitation of Brother Leo's life of Giles in its original form. So much for the early sources. From these, the

---

[14] See "Analecta Bolland.," t. xxi (1902), p. 122. See also Sabatier: "Actus B. Francisci" (Paris, 1902), p. lxviii, Goetz: "Die Quellen zur Geschichte," etc. (Gotha, 1904), p. 98, and Fr. Gisbert Menge, l. c., pp. ix-xv. Of the fifty-nine numbers comprising the "Life of Giles" inserted in the "Chronica XXIV General.," 1-4, 33-36, 57 and 58 are found in the short life edited by Fr. Lemmens.

[15] See "Acta SS.," April, t. iii (edit. Noviss., 1866), pp. 222-228.

[16] See "Doc. Ant. Francis.," pars i, p. 15.

"Actus B. Francisci,"[17] Bartholomew of Pisa,[18] Wadding,[19] and others, have transcribed excerpts; hence what such secondary sources record about Blessed Giles need hardly be reckoned with.

Premising these somewhat dry details, we may pass on to the life of

BLESSED GILES

The life story of Blessed Giles takes us back to the very cradle of the Franciscan Order. It was in the third year of St. Francis's conversion[20] that followers began to gather round the man of God. The first of them was Bernard of Quintavalle — the "venerable" Bernard as St. Bonaventure[21] and Dante[22] call him — a

---

[17] This compilation, which dates from the first half of the fourteenth century, contains among other things most of the Latin text of the traditional "Fioretti." See "Actus," ed. Sabatier, and compare Chaps. 45, 46, 47, and 44 with Nos. 20, 21, 22 and 41 of the life of Giles in the "Chron. XXIV General."

[18] See his "De Conformitate" (Milan edition, 1510), VIII, p. ii, fol. liii a ff. "In Perusio." Although several numbers are here omitted from the life contained in "Chron. XXIV General.," the text of the latter is easily discernible.

[19] See "Annales Minorum," t. iv (ed. 2da, Rome, 1732), pp. 182 ff. Wadding appears to have followed an Italian version of the Latin life inserted in the "Chron. XXIV General." in which the fifty-nine numbers comprising the latter are divided into seventy-two.

[20] See "I Cel.," § 21 (ed. d'Alençon) and "III Soc." § 27 (ed. Faloci).

[21] "Leg. Major," c. 3.

[22] Paradiso, c. xi.

rich and respectable Assisian. The second was Peter Catana or Cattaneo, a Canon of St. Rufino, the cathedral of Assisi. Third in order comes Giles, the subject of our present sketch,[23] "a simple and God fearing man," as Celano [24] describes him.

The history of Giles's conversion is short and simple. The fact that two such leading townsmen as Bernard and Peter had actually embraced Francis's strange mode of life had set all Assisi talking. No sooner had the news reached the ears of Giles — for he had been absent at the time — than he conceived an ardent desire to follow their example. Next morning he arose betimes, and after a fervent prayer at the Church of San Giorgio [25] — for it was St. George's feast day — he set out hurriedly to seek out Francis and his companions. Coming to a crossroads and not knowing which way to turn he paused to ask for guidance from above, when St. Francis, emerging from a wood whither he had retired to pray, met him. Giles, throwing himself at the feet of the Seraphic Founder, begged for the love of God to be allowed to join his holy company. The answer of St. Francis is characteristic. "Dearest," he replied, "God has bestowed on

---

[23] Giles is the more common English form of the Latin Aegidius, as in Italian Gilio is used for Egidio, and in French Gilles for Egide.

[24] "I Cel.," § 25.

[25] Now within the Church of Santa Chiara. See Cristofani, "Delle Storie d'Assisi," vol. i, p. 172.

thee a great gift. If the emperor came to
Assisi and wished to choose one of the townsmen as his knight or chamberlain, many indeed would desire to be selected. How much
the more oughtest thou to be glad, seeing that
the Lord hath picked thee from among them
all, and called thee to His own court." Then
raising Giles from the ground St. Francis led
him by the hand and, calling Brother Bernard,
said: "The Lord hath sent us a good Brother,"
and with joyous hearts they sat down to eat
together. And when they had eaten whatever
there was in the hut, St. Francis started with
Giles to Assisi in quest of some cloth to make
him a habit. On their way they met a poor
woman who begged an alms. "Let us, my
Brother," said the Saint, "give her thy man-
tle." Giles obeyed so gladly that it seemed to
him as if he saw this alms fly swiftly to heaven,
and in spirit, says the legend, he flew straight
into heaven after it. But when he was finally
arrayed in the poor habit St. Francis had procured for him, words failed Giles altogether
to make known the joy he felt in his heart.[26]
Authors are divided as to the exact date upon
which this took place. That it was upon 23
April — just one week after Bernard and Peter
joined Francis — is certain, but whether in the
year 1208 or 1209 is not so evident. The solu-
tion of this question hinges upon the determina-

---

[26] See "Chron. XXIV. General.," l. c., pp. 74, 76.

tion of the exact time when St. Francis went to Rome to solicit the approbation of his Rule.

Let me hasten to say that this latter question is by no means so definitely settled in favor of 1210 as M. Sabatier's conclusions [27] might lead us to imply. Many difficulties still remain. The year 1209 has in its favor much probability. The arguments adduced by Fr. Quinctianus Müller [28] and Mr. Carmichael,[29] among others, in support of the earlier date, are conformable alike to ancient tradition [30] and to modern chronology.[31] If, however, Wadding, Papini, Sabatier, and others are right in contending for 1210 as the year in which the first Rule of the Friars Minor was approved by Innocent III "vivae vocis oraculo," [32] then 1209 would appear to have been the year of Giles's reception. This is the date set down by the Quaracchi editors.[33]

[27] "Vie de S. François," p. 100.

[28] "Anal. Francis.," t. iii, p. 6, n. 4.

[29] See his article "The Date of the Foundation of the Order" in "Franciscan Annals," October, 1906.

[30] See "Anal. Francis.," t. iii, p. 713; also rubric in Breviarium Romano-Seraph., in festo S. Raphaelis Archangeli (16 April).

[31] See "Appunti Critici sulla cronologia della vita di S. Franc.," published in the "Oriente Serafico" (Assisi, 1895) an. VII, p. 101 f. and reprinted in the "Miscell. Frances.," vol. ix, p. 88 f.

[32] See Wadding, ad an. 1210, n. 1 f.; also "Leg. III Soc.," ed. Civezza-Domenichelli, p. 23; Panfilo: "Storia Compendiosa," t. i, c. 2; and Menge, l. c., p. 115.

[33] "Dicta B. Aegidii," Praefatio, p. vi.

Not only when, but also where, Giles's reception took place is a matter of dispute in so far as it involves the still controverted question as to the place inhabited by the Poverello and his first companions before the approbation of the Rule. It is not necessary for the purpose of this sketch to consider in detail the long series of controversies about the respective claims of Rivotorto and the Porziuncula, controversies which, for the rest, as too often happens in such cases, have generated at times more heat than light.[34] But it may conduce to a better understanding of the present question to give in parallel columns the apparently conflicting passages from the Life of Blessed Giles inserted in the "Chronica XXIV Generalium" and from the shorter one edited more recently:

I	II
Versus hospitale leprosorum (Aegidius) se transtulit ubi tunc beatus Franciscus in quodam tugurio derelicto cum fratre Bernardo da Quintavalle et fratre Petro Cathanii morabatur.[35]	Dirigit (Aegidius) gressus suos ad ecclesiam sanctae Mariae de Portiuncula ubi beatus Franciscus cum dictis duobus fratribus morabatur.[36]

---

[34] For an excellent statement of the whole question, see Mr. Carmichael's article "The First Franciscan Convent" in the "Downside Review" for April, 1902, pp. 1-17. An Italian translation of this article by Prof. Pietro Vigo appeared in the "Miscellanea Francescana," vol. ix, fasc. i (1902), pp. 22-29.

[35] "Anal. Francis.," t. iii, p. 75.

[36] "Doc. Ant. Francis.," pars i, p. 39.

Introduction xvii

Papini, misled as it seems by the first of these texts, holds that Giles was received in the abandoned hut at Rivotorto [37] and M. Sabatier, relying on the more explicit testimony of his own "Speculum Perfectionis," [38] is of the same opinion.[39] On the other hand, Father Leonard Lemmens [40] and Mr. Carmichael,[41] conformably to the second text and following Celano,[42] and St. Bonaventure,[43] — according to whom St. Francis did not abide at Rivotorto until after his return from Rome — place the reception of Giles at the Porziuncula. On the whole, this second opinion — which has in its favor the traditional "Legenda III Sociorum," [44] — seems to me altogether more probable. But as I write habitually — like the medieval scribes — under the correction of all "witty and solemn doctors," I shall be glad to learn if I am mistaken in this conclusion or any other herein expressed. Meanwhile we may hold that Giles was admitted to a share

---

[37] "La Storia di S. Francesco," l. c.
[38] "In primordio religionis cum maneret apud Rigum Tortum cum duobus fratribus quos tunc tantum habebat, ecce quidam nomine Aegidius qui fuit tertius frater, venit ad ipsum ut reciperet vitam ejus." — "Spec. Perf.," ed. Sabatier, c. 36.
[39] Sabatier, l. c., p. 263.
[40] "Doc. Ant. Francis.," pars iii, p. 8.
[41] "Franciscan Annals," l. c., p. 312.
[42] "I Cel.," §§ 21 and 42.
[43] "Leg. Major," c. 2 and 4.
[44] "Leg. III Soc.," § 32.

in the poverty of St. Francis at the Porziuncula on 23 April, 1209.

It is much to be regretted that the story of Giles's life prior to this date is unknown to us. No doubt it would be easy to sketch an imaginary outline of it in harmony with the established facts of his after-life, but conjecture is not history, and we are reduced to silence seeing that the early sources to which we might look for some details of Giles's parentage and early years say nothing on this head. Not indeed that this need surprise us. The purely historical features of a saint's life, everything in fact which illustrated only the human side — features which we have come to regard as almost essential to a complete grasp of the subject — such things were of little or no interest to the thirteenth century hagiographer. Moreover, the medieval legends of the saints were mostly, as their name implies, intended for reading in the refectory. Hence their comparative disregard of all save what actually tends to edify. Remembering this — and how much depends upon the point of view — we must not look for a methodical account of the actions of Blessed Giles in the Leonine life as it has come down to us. Indeed it is no easy task to follow the details this life gives in anything like chronological order. In striving to do this, we may, if only for the sake of greater clearness, divide Giles's life after his reception by St. Francis into two periods — one of action, the other of contemplation.

The first may be said to have begun on the very morrow of Giles's reception when in company with St. Francis he set out for the Marches of Ancona. They followed no fixed route but went along as the spirit moved them, like children careless of the day, St. Francis taking the lead and often singing aloud in broken French the praises of God. "Our Order," he said to Giles, "shall be like to the fisherman who casteth his nets into the water, catching a great multitude of fishes, and who keepeth the large ones, leaving the little ones in the water." And Giles, seeing the small number of the Friars, marvelled at this prediction. And when occasion offered, St. Francis would deliver a short exhortation to the bystanders urging charity and penance. After he had concluded, Giles would add in effect: "Ye must believe what my Brother Francis telleth you: the advice he giveth you is very good." Then without further ado they would resume their journey rejoicing, careless of the insults they received by the way. Indeed the honor shown them by some troubled them more. "We are losing our true glory," said Giles to Francis, "since we receive glory from men." Having, after this fashion, evangelized the greater part of the Province of the

Marches, St. Francis and Giles returned to the Porziuncula.[45]

The year following, Giles accompanied St. Francis to Rome, and, after the approval of the Rule by Innocent III, he received the ecclesiastical tonsure together with the holy Patriarch and his ten other companions.[46] Some time after,[47] Giles set out for Spain on a pilgrimage to the shrine of St. James at Compostella, one of the most famous in Christendom. During this journey he suffered untold hunger because of the prevailing famine, and esteemed himself lucky in finding some unthreshed beans to eat. Meeting a man poorer than himself, Giles cut off his capuche and gave it to the stranger as an alms, going bareheaded himself in consequence for some twenty days. At Ficarollo, in Lombardy, on his way back, a man called Giles as if to give him an alms, but instead put dice in his outstretched hand and invited him to play. "May the Lord forgive thee," replied Giles, unruffled, as he continued his tramp.

[45] For details of this and St. Francis's other traditional journeys in the Marches, see P. Candido Mariotti, O.F.M.: "I Primordi dell' Ordine Minoritico nelle Marche."

[46] See Bonav. "Leg. Major," c. 3, n. 10, and "Leg. III Soc.," § 52. It is therefore an error to describe Giles thenceforth as a lay brother.

[47] Probably 1211-1212. See Wadding: "Annales," ad annum 1212, n. 57.

Introduction xxi

Later on [48] he set off for Jerusalem to venerate the Holy Sepulchre, being the first Minorite to set foot in Palestine.[49] While awaiting a vessel at Brindisi he procured a water-pot and peddled water about the town, thus earning the necessaries of life for himself and his companion. And on his way back, likewise detained some days at S. Jean d'Acre in Syria,[50] he was at pains to procure food for them both by making rush baskets and by carrying the dead to the cemetery. And when such means failed him, he had " recourse to the table of the Lord, begging alms from door to door." [51] In the intervals of his work, and sometimes in the midst of it, Giles preached to the people — if preaching it can be called — exhorting them to the fear and love of God.

After his return to Italy, Giles visited Monte Gargano, consecrated to St. Michael the Arch-

[48] About 1215. See Wadding, l. c., ad an. 1215, n. 35.
[49] See P. Girolamo Golubovich, O.F.M., " Biblioteca Bio-Bibliografica della Terra Santa," t. i (1906), p. 105. The Friars Minor have been established in Jerusalem since about 1220.
[50] The Latin reads "in civitate Achon." Wadding and two codices of the " Chron. XXIV General." wrongly read " Anconae " and the early editions of the " De Conformitate " no less erroneously read " Achaiae." But all the other eleven MSS. of the " Chron. XXIV General." and the oldest known codex of the "De Conformitate," preserved in the archives at La Verna, rightly read " Achon." See P. Girolamo Golubovich, l. c.
[51] These words, quoted in the early Life, are taken from the Testament of St. Francis. See " Writings of St. Francis," Dolphin Press, Phila. 1906, p. 84.

angel, and the shrine of St. Nicholas at Bari, both in Apulia.[52] During a subsequent sojourn in Rome [53] Giles lived, as usual, by the labors of his hands. After hearing Mass early in the morning, he would go to a wood some eight miles from the city and having gathered a faggot of fuel would carry it back and exchange it for bread and other things needful for the life of the body. When the vintage came round Giles helped to gather grapes for the peasants and trod them in the winepress, and when the corn was being cut he went with the rest of the poor to glean the ears, but if any one offered him a handful of grain he said: "I have no granary wherein I could store it"; and for the rest he gave away the ears he gathered, for the love of God. He once engaged to beat a walnut tree for a man who could find no one else willing, because the tree was so tall and hard to climb. The share of nuts that fell to Giles's lot was so great that he took off his habit and made a sack of it to hold the nuts, which he distributed among the poor on his way back to the convent. Although ever ready to turn his hand to any job, Giles rarely hired himself out for the whole day; or if he did, he

[52] It is difficult to determine whether or not Giles returned to the Porziuncula before undertaking this pilgrimage. See "Anal. Francis.," t. iii, p. 77, n. 7.

[53] In 1212 St. Francis acquired for his Friars the building in Trastevere where the convent of S. Francesco a Ripa now stands.

made it a condition to have sufficient time to recite his canonical hours.

Giles's earliest biographer also tells us of the fervor with which he always heard Mass, of the ardent devotion with which he received Holy Communion every Sunday and on the principal festivals, and of the reverence in which he held all ecclesiastical laws and regulations. Moreover, if any one spoke to him of the Church, he would exclaim in accents of eager love: "O Holy Mother Roman Church, we foolish and miserable ones do not know thee or thy goodness. Thou teachest us the way of salvation; thou preparest and showest us the path by which if any one walketh, his feet shall not stray but attain to glory."

Once returning from a dense wood with a bundle of twigs a priest whom he met called Giles a hypocrite, which grieved him so sorely that he could scarce refrain from tears. Asked by another Friar the cause of his weeping, Giles said: "Because I am a hypocrite, as a certain priest told me." "Believest thou this," said the other, "because he said so?" Giles answered: "I believe, because it is a priest that said it; for I do not believe that priests lie." Whereupon the other said: "Father, the opinions of men, who are liable to err, are often at variance with those of God." On hearing which Giles's peace of mind was restored. While staying at the monastery of the Quattrosanti, near the Lateran, Giles helped the baker in his work and also drew water for the monks. One day, when he was returning with water from the fountain of San Sesto, a man asked him for a drink. Giles answered: "How can I give you a drink and bring what is left to the monks?" Whereupon the other, much excited, said many hard things. Having returned to the monastery Giles procured a pitcher and filling it at the fountain carried it to the house of the irate man, saying: "Drink, brother, and give what remains to whomsoever thou pleasest."

While a guest of Cardinal Nicholas of Clairveaux at Rieti, Giles was once kept indoors because of stormy weather, so he spent his time sweeping the house and polishing the knives, and when his host murmured not a little at this conduct, Giles answered simply in the words of Holy Writ: "For thou shalt eat the labors of thy hands: blessed art thou, and it shall be well with thee."[54] From the Cardinal's house Giles withdrew with a companion to pass the Lent in solitude in the deserted Church of St. Laurence on a hill above Deruta,[55] whence because of a heavy snowstorm they could not go out to seek alms and would

---

[54] Ps. 127 : 2.
[55] According to Wadding, a Franciscan convent was erected here in 1263, which was subsequently suppressed and destroyed.

surely have famished in consequence, had not the Lord inspired a certain man named Benincasa to seek them out and provide for their needs during the remaining days of their retreat.

When at the second General Chapter, held at the Porziuncula in 1219,[56] St. Francis decided to send forth his Friars to evangelize the nations, Giles was assigned to labor for the conversion of Mohammedan Africa. But no sooner had he and his fellow missionaries landed at Tunis than a certain Moor, famed as a fervent disciple of Mohammed, began to cry out: "Infidels have come amongst us who seek to attack our prophet and his law. Go forth, therefore, and put them to death." The whole populace was soon up in arms and the Christian residents, fearing a general massacre, forced Giles and his companions by violence to reëmbark for Italy.

A keen observer of men and manners, Giles picked up in the course of his travels much knowledge and experience, many "wise saws and modern instances," which he afterwards turned to good account. He had already besought St. Francis to assign him to some place of abode — for during several years he does not seem to have been attached to any particular community. St. Francis, who knew his

[56] See Wadding, l. c., ad an. 1219, n. 34, and P. Girolamo Golubovich, l. c., p. 91.

man, and realized that to coop Giles up in any
one place would have been to waste his talents
and energies, replied: "Thou mayest go where
thou wishest." But Giles, "being unable to
quiet his spirit in so much liberty," persisted
in his request and was sent finally to the
hermitage at Fabriano.[57] From thenceforth
Giles's journeyings did not extend beyond the
Marches, Umbria, and Tuscany.

When, in 1226, he heard that St. Francis was
dangerously ill, Giles hastened to the Porziuncula and was present during the last moments
of his beloved Father. So, too, when many
years later Bernard of Quintavalle [58] lay dying,
Giles came to visit him. "Sursum corda,
Brother Bernard, Sursum corda," he exclaimed
on seeing the sick man. And Brother Bernard,
all aglow at this greeting, ordered that they
should prepare for Giles a suitable solace
wherein he might give himself over to contemplation, and this was done.

Unlike Bernard of Quintavalle, Leo, and
others of the early "Companions," Giles kept
aloof from the lamentable controversies within

[57] According to Bartholomew of Pisa and the Bollandist MS. this was in 1214. On this hermitage see P.
Luigi da Fabriano: "Cenni Cronologico-biografici della
Osservante Provincia Picena" (1887), p. 21, and P. Conrad Eubel: "Provinciale Ordinis Minorum" (1892), p. 67.

[58] That Bernard was living at Siena in 1241 we know
from Salimbene: "Chron.," p. 11. That he was dead in
1246 seems clear from the Letter of the "Three Companions" to Crescentius.

the Order which took place after St. Francis's death about the observance of the Rule, and during which the abettors of laxity waged desperate war on the "zelanti." When Leo came to tell him that a magnificent basilica was about to be erected at Assisi and that a marble urn had been set up on the Colle d'Inferno by order of Brother Elias to receive offerings toward its construction, Giles sighed: "Even if it should be as long as from here to Assisi,"[59] he said, "one corner is enough for me to live in." Later on, hearing of the disobedience and excommunication of the ill-starred Elias, Giles threw himself upon the ground and lay there. "I want to get as low as possible," he replied, when asked why he acted thus, "since he fell only because of his leap." "Let me lie," he was wont to exclaim afterwards; "if I do not rise, I cannot fall."

His devotion to St. Francis subsequently impelled Giles to visit Assisi; and after the Friars there had shown him over the large convent they had built, he said to them ironically: "I tell you, my Brothers, there is now but one thing lacking — ye should have wives." At which remark those present were not a little scandalized. But Giles said: "After having thus discarded poverty, it would be but a short step to discard chastity."

[59] This interview seems to have taken place at Perugia.

On one occasion, when Giles was visiting the Poor Ladies at St. Damian's, it happened that an English Friar, a Master in Theology, was preaching there. If we may believe a number of early writers of the Order, this Englishman was none other than the great "Doctor Irrefragabilis," Alexander of Hales himself.[60] Be this as it may, his discourse appears to have been a trifle long; at all events Giles was bored. "Stop, Master!" he exclaimed in fervor of spirit, "for I want to preach." He did so, and poured forth eloquent words. Then, having said his say, he concluded: "Now continue, Brother, the sermon thou hast begun." And the Master again obeyed. At all of which St. Clare was exceedingly edified, for Giles's aim, it seems, was to test the theologian's humility. He had observed, we are told, a decrease of simplicity in several friars who had studied at Paris. It was manifestly against this danger that Giles inveighed when he exclaimed: "O Paris, Paris, thou art ruining the Order of St. Francis!" — a plaint which afterwards found an echo in a familiar satire of Jacopone:[61]

[60] See "Anal. Francis.," t. iii, p. 81, n. 6. See also P. Hilarin Felder, O. Cap.: "Geschichte der Wissenschaftlichen Studien im Franziskanerorden" (1904), p. 177 f.

[61] "Le poesie spirituali del B. Jacopone da Todi, con le scolie ed annotationi di Fra Francesco Tresatti da Lugnano," l. 1, satira 10 (Venetia, 1617), 43.

> Tal'è, qual'è, tal'è,
> Non c'è religione
> Mal vedemmo Parisi,
> Che n'ha destrutto Assisi
> Con la lor lettoria
> L'hanno messo in mala via.

But if the learning of some friars displeased Giles, that of others inspired him with esteem. "My Father," he once said to St. Bonaventure, "God hath laden thee with many graces in giving thee that knowledge which helpeth thee to praise Him. But we poor ignorant creatures, how can we correspond with His goodness?" When the Saint replied that if God had given man His love alone it would suffice, "What," exclaimed Giles, "can an ignorant man love God as much as a learned one?" "Certainly," replied the Seraphic Doctor; "a poor little old woman can love God as much or more than a Master in Theology." Whereupon Giles, running to the garden wall overlooking the town, cried out to a poor woman who was passing: "O poor little old woman, foolish and ignorant as thou art, love the Lord God and thou mayest be greater than Brother Bonaventure." The Seraphic Doctor held Giles in special veneration, and thanked God for having permitted him to live at a time when he could converse with such a man. "I have often seen him with my own eyes," he writes,[62] "so rapt in God,

---

[62] "Leg. Major," c. 3, n. 4. See also "Sermo I in Sabbato Sancto" in "Opera omnia," t. ix, p. 269.

that he might be said rather to live amongst men the life of an angel than of man."

It was in the hermitage at Fabriano [63] that the "hand of the Lord was laid upon him," [64] and that he "felt his soul slip out of his body," in the first of that long series of ecstasies which continued with very visible, yet still tranquil, increase until his death. We need not hope to follow Giles during these ecstasies; he mounted a rarefied atmosphere where we cannot breathe. In 1226, after he had kept the Lent of St. Martin with very great devotion at Cetona, near Chiusi in Tuscany, he was favored with the spiritual presence of St. Francis himself. At the same hermitage our Lord appeared to Giles on Christmas eve, and he continued in ecstasy with little intermission until Epiphany. He was afterward wont to say that he had been born four times: at his natural birth, at his Baptism, at his entry into religion, and, finally, on the day of this vision. "Thou didst once tell me," remarked Brother Andrew of Burgundy,[65] the familiar and persistent companion of Giles, "that when Christ appeared to thee at Cetona, thy faith was taken away. . . . Having no faith, what wouldst thou do if thou wert a priest and had to say

---

[63] Probably as early as 1215.
[64] IV Kings 3 : 15.
[65] On Brother Andrew, see Wadding, l. c., ad an. 1282, n. 20, and 40; also "Anal. Francis.," t. iii, p. 100.

Mass? How couldst thou say 'I believe in one God'?" And Giles with a joyful face sang aloud, "I *know* one God, the Father Almighty." "What would ye do, sons," he exclaimed after an all-night rapture at Agello near Trasimene, "if ye saw the greater things? He who hath not seen the greater things believeth everything to be little." "Blessed is the man who knoweth how to keep the secrets of God," was all Giles would say with reference to what he had seen and heard on another like occasion. But Giles earned his raptures by hard-won victories. The assaults of the demon increased in proportion to his visions, so much so that often on retiring to his cell for the night he would say with a sigh: "Now I await my martyrdom."

After the vision of Cetona, where Giles saw our Lord Himself with his fleshly eyes, he scarcely ever left his cell. "He remaineth," said Bernard of Quintavalle once, "like a *domicella* in her chamber." "Go forth among men," urged the latter jokingly to Giles; "talk with them and procure bread and other necessaries for the Friars." "Brother Bernard," replied Giles, "it is not given to every man as to Bernard of Quintavalle to eat his food on the wing."

When Giles did go abroad, the mere mention in his hearing of the word "Paradise" —whispered in his ear perhaps by a mischievously prompted small boy — was sufficient to throw the holy man into a spiritual rapture. Hence the Friars who came to converse with him were obliged carefully to avoid alluding to heaven. If any one spoke to him of God, he would kiss the flowers, trees, and stones — for he seemed to see God in all creatures by a certain heavenly and sweet light.

On one occasion, when Gregory IX visited the convent outside Perugia, where Giles was, the Pontiff was a witness to the long ecstasies of the servant of God, but was unable to converse with him. He therefore invited Giles to dine with him on the morrow, but soon after he had come Giles fell into a rapture, and remained immovable. "Verily," exclaimed the Pope, "if thou die before me I will ask no other miracle to canonize thee."[66] Next day, when the Pope expressed a desire to have a few words from Giles that should inform him what he ought to be — "Holy Father," said Giles, after some persuasion — for he was reluctant to advise the Pope — "keep thy spiritual eyes pure: the right one for contemplating heavenly things, the left for judging rightly the world that you have to govern." This was about 1235.

It would be a mistake, however, to suppose that Brother Giles went through life without

---

[66] Murillo has made this scene the subject of a striking picture.

Introduction xxxiii

ever descending to the level of our ordinary existence. An incident recorded of his sojourn at Cetona suffices to prove the contrary. Being an enthusiastic gardener, he had cultivated there a patch of beautiful cabbages. One day a certain Friar, wishing to try Giles, entered the garden armed with a big sword and began to work havoc among the vegetables. Whereupon, Giles calling aloud, laid hands on the intruder and put him by force out of the garden. "O Brother Giles," said the Friar, "where is thy patience and thy sanctity?" To which Giles replied with a sigh: "Pardon me, Brother, but thy invasion was so sudden I was not armed and had no time to fortify myself." This story is interesting as illustrating the human side of the great ecstatic. And the school of hagiography which overlooks this side, is, to say the least, most discouraging, in so far as it places the saints on a pedestal quite above the reach of human endeavor. As a consequence, we admire them, as the inhabitants of Umbria and the Marches admire their mountains — "from afar off and without the idea ever occurring to them of making the ascent."

The story of how St. Louis, King of France, came to visit Brother Giles is told in the "Fioretti," [67] and the narrative is so redolent

---

[67] See "Floretum S. Francisci." (Ed. Sabatier), cap. xxiv, pp. 149-150.

of the true *Umbria mystica* that no apology need be made for quoting it in full: —

"St. Louis, King of France, went on a pilgrimage to visit the different sanctuaries in the world. Having heard of the fame and sanctity of Brother Giles, who was one of the first companions of St. Francis, he determined in his heart to go and visit him in person; for which object he set out for Perugia, where the said Brother then lived. He arrived at the convent-gate as if he had been a poor, unknown pilgrim, and asked with great importunity for Brother Giles, without telling the porter who it was who wished to see him; and the porter went to Brother Giles, and told him there was a pilgrim at the gate who asked for him. And the Lord having revealed to Brother Giles that the pilgrim was the King of France, he left his cell in haste and ran to the gate without asking any questions. They both knelt down and embraced each other with great reverence and many outward signs of love and charity, as if a long friendship had existed between them, though they had never met before in their lives. Neither of them spoke a word; and after remaining clasped in each other's arms for some time they separated in silence, St. Louis to continue his journey, and Brother Giles to return to his cell. As the king departed, one of the Friars inquired of one of the persons who accompanied him who it was who had embraced Brother Giles, and he answered that it was Louis, King of France; and when the others heard this they were sorrowful because Brother Giles had not spoken to him, and, giving vent to their grief, they said: "O Brother Giles, why hast thou been so uncivil as not to say a word to such a holy king, who hath come from France to see thee, and hear from thee some good words?" Brother Giles answered: "Beloved Brothers, be not surprised at this, as neither I could say a word to him nor he to me; for no sooner had we embraced each other than the light of Divine Wisdom revealed his heart to me and mine to him; and by a divine operation we saw into each other's hearts, and knew far better what we had to say than if we had explained in words that which we experienced in our souls. The tongue of man revealeth so imperfectly the secret mysteries of God that it would have been to us rather a hindrance than a consolation. Know then that the king went away satisfied with me, and greatly comforted in mind."

"Of all of which story," writes Ruskin,[68] "not a word, of course, is credible by any rational person. Certainly not." Unfortunately, as the Bollandists noted long ago,[69]

---

[68] "Mornings in Florence — Before the Soldan." P. 89.
[69] See "Acta SS.," Aug. V. Comm. Praev., § lxii. See also Le Monnier, "History of St. Francis," p. 85.

nothing authorizes us to think that St. Louis ever passed through Italy at all. So far as is known, his visit to Perugia is recorded only in the "Fioretti."[70] Some attribute the story to a confusion between the French king and his namesake, St. Louis of Toulouse, who is still patron of Perugia.[71] In any event, as the author of "Mornings in Florence" adds: "The spirit which created the story is an entirely indisputable fact in the history of Italy and of mankind. Whether St. Louis and Brother Giles ever knelt together in the streets of Perugia matters not a whit. That a king and a poor monk could be conceived to have thoughts of each other which no words could speak, and that indeed the king's tenderness and humility made such a tale credible to the people — that is what you have to meditate on here." This is well said. Umbrian literature alone could have left us such a picture.

It has been said of St. Francis, with pardonable warmth, that he entered into glory in his lifetime. The same in measure and degree is true of Giles. His holy life and, above all, his frequently recurring ecstasies had surrounded him with a halo of mysterious veneration, while his fame as a speaker of

[70] Salimbene, who has so much to say about St. Louis in his "Chronicle," is silent on the subject.

[71] See "The Story of Perugia," p. 199.

"good words" led many men of all sorts and conditions to toil up the steep, tiled way — now overgrown with daisies — which leads from Perugia to Monteripido, where his later years were passed. Giles spoke to one and all with apostolic freedom, for he was no respecter of persons and never minced his words.

Two cardinals, who had come to visit Giles, asked him on leaving to pray for them. "Why should I pray for you," he replied, "since you have more faith and hope than I have?" "How is that?" they asked. "Because with so much riches and honor and worldly prosperity you hope to be saved, whilst I, with so much misery and adversity, fear to be damned!" Two Friars, expelled from Sicily by Frederic II, came to see Giles and spoke of the emperor as a persecutor. "You are sinning against Frederic," he cried out, clinching his fists, "that greatest of sinners. Since he hath done you much good you ought rather to pray God to soften his heart than to murmur against him; he hath not expelled you from your country, for if you be true Friars Minor you have no country." He was sharper still with a certain Friar who came exultingly to tell him that he had had a vision of hell and could not see a single Friar there. "I believe it," said Giles with a strange smile. "How is it?" asked the visionary. "It is, my son," answered Giles, "because thou didst not go down deep enough."

Another Friar, who came in quest of spiritual counsel, found Giles in better humor. "I will tell thee what to do," he said, "but I want to sing it." Taking a stick he began to saw with it, as if fiddling, and running about the garden, he kept singing: "Una uni, una uni," but said nothing else. "Do this," he concluded, "and then thou wilt please God." And the other, failing to understand, Giles explained: "*Una* et sola anima sine intermissione et medio *uni* soli Deo committenda est."[72]

But Giles was nothing if not original. At another time, while the Lady Jacoba of Settesoli[73] was visiting Giles, Brother Gerardino, "a very spiritual man," called to see him. Gerardino, wishing to draw out Giles, sought to prove by twelve arguments that man is incapable of free action. "Can you sing, Brother Gerardino?" asked Giles when the logician had concluded. Then, drawing from his sleeve a small lute made of cornstalk, such as boys use, and beginning with the first string

---

[72] The play on words is almost obscured in the English: Our one and only soul is to be committed without interruption or go-between to the one and only God.

[73] On the Lady Jacoba, see Wadding, "Annales" ad an. 1212, n. 34. See also the interesting brochure by Père Edouard d'Alençon, O.M. Cap., "Frère Jacqueline" (Paris, 1899).

Introduction xxxix

and continuing on each string of the lute, Giles in words of music quashed and confuted the twelve reasons of poor Gerardino.[74]

When some one came to tell Giles that he wished by all means to become a religious, he said: "In that case, go quickly and kill thy parents." Aghast at this unlooked-for advice, the would-be religious said tearfully: "Oh! Brother Giles, how could I be guilty of such a crime!" "O simpleton!" retorted Giles, "not to know that I meant the sword of the spirit, for he who doth not hate his father and mother cannot be my disciple."[75]

Brother Gratian, the constant and devoted companion of Giles, once asked the latter to tell him how he could please God most. "Go and hang thyself" was the answer. Having brooded over this curious counsel for many days, Gratian begged Giles to interpret it, which he did thus: "A man who is hanging by the neck, though not in heaven is yet lifted up from the earth and always looketh downwards. This should be thy attitude."

This same Brother Gratian once announced to Giles that five Provincials of the Order

---

[74] There is a great diversity of spelling in the name of this Friar among the early MSS. See "Anal. Francis.," t. iii, p. 102, n. 3. It is probable that Giles's visitor on this occasion was none other than Gerardo, or Gerardino of Borgo San Donnino, author of the famous "Introduction to the Eternal Gospel."

[75] See Luke 14:26.

had arrived to see him. "O Brother mine!" exclaimed Giles, "O beautiful Brother! O Brother of love! build me a castle which shall have neither stone nor iron." Saying which he was rapt in God. Needless to add that in proportion as his visions and ecstasies increased the world had less hold on Giles. No longer did he bewail his failure to attain the martyr's crown at Tunis. On the contrary. "I do not wish I had died then," he would say, "I do not desire to die a better death than that of contemplation." His wish was fulfilled. On Saturday, 22 April, 1262,[76] Giles passed from earth without struggle as one who had grown used to being absent from the body, and entered heaven at last as a conqueror.

When it became noised abroad that Giles was near his end, the Perugians, knowing that he wished to be buried at the Porziuncula, placed soldiers around the Convent of Monteripido to prevent his departure. They were determined to retain the relics of so great a saint at any cost. This rivalry between different towns for possession of the bodies of

[76] This date is based upon the hypothesis that Giles received the habit 23 April, 1209 (see above, p. xv.) and lived fifty-three years in the Order. Ample facilities for verifying it will be found in Menge, l. c., pp. 114-115. But Frs. Quinctianus Müller ("Anal. Francis.," t. iii, p. 114, n. 4) and Golubovich (l. c., p. 103) contend for 1261. See also Wadding, "Annales," t. iv, ad an. 1262, n. 3, p. 182, and Papini, l. c., i, 195.

Introduction xli

holy men and women was a curious characteristic of medieval piety. The Perugians afford a striking example of this tendency. We all remember how they hovered along the road by which St. Francis was borne to Assisi during his last illness, determined if possible to carry him off by force so that he might die in their city.[77] Nearly a century later the same Perugians stole the body of Blessed Conrad of Offida from Bastia, and bore it off to San Francesco.[78] "Tell the Perugians," said the dying Giles, when he heard of their precautions, "that the bells shall never ring for my canonization, or because of any great miracle of mine; no sign will be given them except that of Jonas." "Even if he should not be canonized," they answered, "we will keep him." And they did.

His remains, after lying in state for a full month in the Convent Al Monte, were conveyed with great pomp to Perugia and interred in the Church of S. Francesco al Prato. Now, when the Perugians were searching for a stone-block out of which to make his tomb, they found a marble sarcophagus on which the history of the prophet Jonas was sculptured, and in this, seeing the verification of his prediction, they buried him. They after-

[77] See Le Monnier, l. c., p. 482.
[78] See "Catalogus Sanctorum Fratrum Minorum," Ed. Lemmens, p. 8.

wards placed a tablet above his tomb in the chapel of the Crispolti, concluding thus: " Gloriatur quidem gemmis India, thure Saba, auro Arabia, Aegyptus sapientia, Italia potentia: nunc igitur Augusta Perusia exultet, gaudeat et glorietur de isto thesauro incomparabili B. Aegidio qui Sacri Minorum Ordinis mirifici aedificii lapis permanet in perpetuum." Salimbene tells us that Giles had prayed in his humility that he might work no miracles after death. But the pious Perugians aver that his prayer was not heard, and the long list of wonders wrought through his intercession, and recorded by the Bollandists,[79] seem to bear them out. They forthwith gave Giles the title of Blessed, and his immemorial cultus was confirmed by Pius VI in 1777.[80] His feast is celebrated on 23 April.[81]

Wadding [82] bears witness to the Perugians' devotion toward Giles in his day; but that devotion, which was waning when Papebroche wrote,[83] has now almost died out. This decline

---

[79] See " Acta SS.," l. c., p. 244–249. This list of miracles wrought within a year of Giles's death appears to have been drawn up by a contemporary.

[80] Giles is the only one of the first companions of St. Francis who has thus far been raised to the honors of the altar. The cause of Beatification of the others is still under way. See " De Causis Beatorum et Servorum Dei Ordinis Minorum " (Quaracchi, 1905), p. 19.

[81] See " Breviarium Romano-Seraphicum," 23 April.

[82] " Annales," ad an. 1262, n. 10.

[83] See " Acta SS.," l. c., p. 221, E.

must no doubt be attributed, at least in part, to external causes. The beautiful Church of S. Francesco, which was built in 1230, almost completely fell in, in 1737, and is now wellnigh in ruins.[84] Giles's remains, which reposed here until 1860, were then, through the united efforts of the Archbishop, Cardinal Pecci, afterwards Pope Leo XIII, and the Minister General of the Conventuals, removed to the archiepiscopal palace. Twenty years later (1880) Monsignor Foschi, Archbishop of Perugia, ordered them to be interred in the Cathedral of S. Lorenzo. Here, in the Chapel of S. Onofrio, which serves as a winter choir, they now repose under the altar, side by side, through a happy coincidence, with the remains of Blessed Conrad of Offida,[85] to whom Giles came after death to teach the secrets of contemplation. Since the suppression of 1860 the Conventuals, into whose care it had passed, have not returned to S. Francesco, nor is there much hope that they will, in view of its present condition, and the little likelihood of its being restored. Hence Giles's remains may lie indefinitely in the cathedral. Surely it would

[84] Its priceless pictures have been removed to the Pinacoteca and other galleries.
[85] See the delightful "Vita Fratris Conradi" in the "Chron. XXIV General.," l. c., pp. 427-428. He died in 1306. Sixteen years later his body, as mentioned above, was carried off by the Perugians from Bastia and interred near that of Giles in S. Francesco al Prato.

seem more appropriate, under the circumstances, that they should repose in the convent of the Friars Minor on Monteripido without the Porta Sant' Angelo.

The cell occupied by Blessed Giles — which has been transformed into a chapel — as well as his little garden, are enclosed within the precincts of this convent, which was built in 1276, through the generosity of James di Coppoli,[86] on the site of the house where he had been "wont most tenderly to entertain the Blessed Brother Giles,"[87] and which rises bare but beautiful on the summit of Monteripido, commanding a superb panorama across the unshadowed Umbrian plain to Assisi, and beyond it to Subasio on whose wooded slopes, around the silent solitude of the Carceri, the grotto once occupied by Giles is still to be seen. It is a natural grotto in the rocky side of the gorge, and measures one metre in width and less than two metres in length.

Among the earliest paintings preserved in the Pinacoteca at Perugia is one of Giles, painted — so tradition tells us — upon an old table upon which his body had lain after

[86] The deed of donation, found by Professor A. Rossi in 1865, has been published in the "Miscellanea Francescana," vol. iv., par. v (1889), pp. 157-159. See also "The Story of Perugia," pp. 197-198.

[87] A silk mill on the lower slope of Monteripido marks the site of the older convent, said to have been founded by St. Francis himself.

death. In the centre of this panel Giles is represented as standing erect, within a niche, surrounded by scenes from his life. One of these, which depicts the meeting with St. Louis,[88] is here reproduced after a pen draw-

ing made in 1777 by Carlo Mariotti and F. Appiani; for the original painting is now so faded and battered as to be barely discernible.

[88] Mrs. de Selincourt in her "Homes of the First Franciscans," p. 126, describes a fresco of Fra Angelico at S. Marco, in Florence, representing this same scene; but I have searched in vain for any other reference to such a fresco, and nothing seems to be known about it at S. Marco.

Perhaps the nearest approach to a "vera effigies" of Blessed Giles that has come down to us is the medallion, by Benozzo Gozzoli, in San Francesco, at Montefalco.[89] A glance at the vigorously painted heads of the first Franciscans there suffices to show that, whereas the likeness of St. Francis is an ideal creation, that of Giles has a characteristic originality about it which seems to bespeak a faithful reproduction of some earlier portrait already traditional.

Be this as it may, we will now proceed, in the second place, to the consideration of the

GOLDEN SAYINGS

of Blessed Giles, which, after all, reveal to us more of his genius and character than any legendary likeness or biographical study. It is in them rather than elsewhere that we must look for the real Giles "in his habit as he lived."

Giles, as we have seen, survived St. Francis more than thirty-five years, and, having lived through the generalates of John Parenti, Elias, Albert of Pisa, Haymo of Faversham, Crescentius of Jesi, Blessed John of Parma, and well into that of St. Bonaventure, he became, as it were, a medium between the second generation of Franciscans and the early time. The

---

[89] See "Franciscan Legends in Italian Art," pp. 108 and 161.

Poverello had, so to say, handed the torch on to Giles, and thus it came to pass that after the master's death men came from all sides to interrogate the disciple, and to hear "the words of life" from the lips of Giles, their especial guardian. It is here we must seek the genesis of the present work. The answers and advice Giles's visitors had received lingered in their memory. They talked over these things among themselves, and committed them to writing, and thus, in the course of time, *sensim sine sensu,* was formed, a collection of spiritual maxims which have been so aptly named the "Dicta," or "Verba Aurea" Beati Aegidii, by the old compilers.

It would be erroneous, however, to infer, on account of their origin, that these "Dicta" are inapplicable save to those to whom they were at first addressed. In spite of their obviously fragmentary and desultory character these "Golden Sayings" contain lessons which we must all needs learn. Never mind, if certain passages have more direct reference to a form of life with which our present unsupernatural habits of life and thought lead to a manifest want of sympathy — that is to say, the contemplative life. Giles's point of view is, on the whole, one which does not depend on time, or place, or state of life. Far different is our age from that in which he lived, and yet the "one thing necessary" is as paramount now as it was then, the same virtues are needed in the twentieth century as in the thirteenth, and we of to-day are no less in danger of declining from the narrow path than were those to whom Giles spoke " good words " in the days of his flesh. And so it happens that these same " good words " are still able to move those who are all unaware of their origin.

The " Golden Sayings " have, therefore, something more than a mere sentimental interest. They possess, moreover, an additional value and interest in so far as they serve to disclose the trend of one aspect of the early Franciscan teaching which has, so far as I know, heretofore received, at least in some quarters, a rather inadequate share of attention — I mean its spiritual side, of which Giles became alike the embodiment and the exponent.

Now one of the chief characteristics of that teaching is its simplicity, wherein, for the rest, lies the cachet of all things truly Franciscan. This trait is faithfully reflected in the " Golden Sayings." He who runs may read, and reading, may comprehend them. These " Sayings," then, embody no formal dissertations or abstract theories. Giles rightly believed that it was preferable to discuss virtue a little less, and to practise it a little more.[90] In other

---

[90] Witness his remarks on this head in chapter iii of the Appendix.

words, his doctrine is the life of St. Francis
and his first companions reduced to the principles of practical virtues, and nothing more.

The high authority of Giles's spiritual teaching may be gathered from the frequency with which his "Sayings" are quoted by ascetical writers, both ancient and modern. St. Bonaventure held them in much esteem, and more than once borrows the language which Giles, speaking from experience, used on contemplation.[91] So does the author of the work "De Septem Gradibus Contemplationis."[92] Yet Giles himself, although he could guide and influence souls so wisely and so well in the highest points of spirituality, was not a theologian in the narrow sense of the word; indeed, he was not even a lettered man; he was, in the words of St. Bonaventure, "homo idiota et simplex." He had not been to Paris, and the culture of his time was closed to him; but he had studied in a fine school when he sat at the feet of St. Francis; and, for the rest, books are not the only font of knowledge, as St. Bonaventure once reminded the Angelic Doctor. What Giles lacked in book learning

---

[91] See below, chapter xiii, and references to St. Bonaventure there indicated.

[92] The MS. copy of this work at the National Library in Florence (Cod. M, 1817, B. 8) begins: "Quidam libellus super septem gradus contemplationis secundum quod ex inspiratione divina sanctus Frater Aegidius invenit." The author of this work is unknown.

was supplied from another source. The constant contemplation of heavenly things, seconded by a perfect purity of life, at the same time that it sharpened Giles's natural faculties, familiarized him with the most profound speculations of the supernatural truths, and the analysis of the human heart.[93] Hence the charm of his spiritual maxims. Although saturated with supernaturalism, they are yet exquisitely human, instinct with common sense, and free from all stiffness or pedantry. In a familiar way, by precept and proverb, by homely instances, by the lessons of experience, Giles treats "vices and virtues, punishment and glory, with brevity of speech,"[94] with a view to converting all men, high and low, and fixing in their hearts the substance and solidity of religious duty. Terse, pithy, and sententious, full of force and unction, his "Sayings" combine a mixture of mystic gravity, pious ardor, and sprightly good nature in which the apothegmatic element prevails and from which the paradoxical is not always absent. Some one asks Giles a question. He replies to it with such vivacity as to arouse and impress his questioner. In a word, Giles has left us in these "Sayings" something of

---

[93] See "Anal. Bolland.," t. xxiv, fasc. iii, p. 410, to which I am indebted for several references.
[94] See Rule of the Friars Minor, chap. 9, "Writings of St. Francis of Assisi," l. c., p. 71.

his own personality which we feel instinctively without being quite able to explain its presence. In them, after six centuries, Giles still speaks — "defunctus adhuc loquitur." It is not hard then to understand the popularity the "Dicta" attained.

But since it is clear from what has been said that Giles wrote nothing himself, a natural query would be: Who first collected his Sayings? To this question no more definite answer can be given than is found in the early MSS. Some codices attribute their collection to Brother Leo,[95] who, as we have seen, wrote Giles's life; others attribute it to Giles's companions,[96] among whom Brothers Gratian, Andrew of Burgundy, and John,[97] are most frequently mentioned in the early legends and chronicles.[98]

---

[95] See below, p. lii.

[96] See below, p. liii.

[97] John seems to have been the companion "per excellentiam." It is to him the Three Companions appeal in their prefatory letter. See "Anal. Francis.," t. iii, p. 74, n. 9; also "Doc. Ant. Francis.," t. iii, p. 17, where several references are given.

[98] It has been suggested (see "Etudes Franciscaines," t. xiv, October, 1905, p. 415) that these companions may perhaps have blended some of their own "sayings" with those of Giles; but, as Fr. Van Ortroy well remarks ("Anal. Bolland.," l. c.), it is not expedient to push literary scruples to extremes in so far as concerns the authenticity of each of the sentences from which this collection is formed. For the rest, as M. Paul Sabatier, speaking of another work, justly observes: "The pious

Whichever may be the correct account, it is certain that the collection dates from the thirteenth century: a codex containing it, and dating at least from the year 1300, is preserved in the Biblioteca Laurenziana at Florence. A great number of other medieval MSS. comprising collections of the "Dicta" are now scattered through various libraries.

I. First among these collections comes the one attributed to Leo. In the MS. it is, for the most part, subjoined to the short Life of Blessed Giles by Brother Leo, which has been edited by Father Lemmens,[99] and is the smallest of all.[100]

Religious who made these compilations were in no degree critics, but in default of scientific principles, they had spiritual discernment."

[99] See "Documenta Ant. Francis.," pars. i, pp. 63-72.

[100] This collection (which shall be referred to hereafter under the figure I) begins "Praevide verba" and ends "propter beatitudinem poena." It may be found in the following codices: (1) Leignitz (Lib. of SS. Peter and Paul, cod. 12, XV cent., fol. 97 r); (2) Oxford (Bodl. Lib. cod. Canon miscell., 525, XIV cent., fol. 145 v); (3) Buda Pest (Nat. Lib. cod. med. aev., lat. 77, XIV-XV cent., fol. 53 r); (4) St. Florian (Austria) (Monast. Lib. Cod. XI, 148 XIV cent., fol., 50 v); (5) Rome (Archiv. of St. Isidore's Coll., cod. 1/73, XIV cent., fol. 90 r); (6) Rome (Nat. Lib. cod. Fondo Vitt. Em., 37, XV cent., fol. 126 r). In the four first mentioned MSS. the collection of the "Dicta" is attributed to Brother Leo as follows: "Thus far we have written some things which Brother Leo the companion of St. Francis noted down." In the St. Isidore cod. 1/73 the word Leo is omitted in this *explicit*.

Introduction liii

II. Much larger and more familiar is a second collection of the "Dicta" attributed to the "companions" of Giles, and found in the well-known fourteenth century compilation of *materia seraphica* known, from the opening words of its prologue, as "Fac secundum exemplar."[101] Bartholomew of Pisa inserted this collection of the "Dicta" in his very remarkable book "De Conformitate,"[102] and it has been published by the Bollandists[103] and others. In this collection of the "Dicta"[104] — as is often the case with early Franciscan codices — we can distinguish a double current, that is, two families or classes of MSS.

The first of these families is represented by the collection found in the compilation "Fac secundum exemplar";[105] the second, which is that followed by Bartholomew of Pisa and

[101] See Sabatier, "Speculum Perfectionis," p. clxxvi, for a description of MSS. containing this collection.

[102] See the Milan edit. of 1510, fruct. viii.

[103] "Acta SS" ad diem 23 Aprilis, De B. Aegidio, pars ii, Aurea Verba.

[104] It begins: "Gratiae Dei et virtutes sunt scala," and shall be referred to hereafter under the figure II.

[105] This collection, which ends "dignus est poenis aeternis," shall be referred to hereafter as A. It may be found in the Leignitz, Oxford, and Buda Pest codices already mentioned, as well as in the fourteenth century Vatican MS. 4354, fol. 112 r, and in the St. Isidore MSS. 1/63 and 1/89. The two last named MSS. have proper endings.

the Bollandists,[106] differs from the first in several details.[107]

III. With a few exceptions all the "Dicta" contained in this two-fold collection are to be found in the Florentine Codex already mentioned,[108] although in somewhat inverted or-

[106] This second collection, which ends "Deus bona sua quae ipse faciat, appropriat," shall be hereafter referred to as B. It may be found in the following MSS.: (1-2) Assisi (Munic. Lib. cod. 590, XIV cent., fol. 16 v, and cod. 191, XIV cent., fol. 146 r); (3) Brussels (Royal Lib. cod. 2620-34, XV cent. (1447), fol. 262 r); (4) Deventer (Athen. Lib. cod. 10 w 5, XIV-XV cent., fol. 121 r); (5) Hague (Royal Lib. cod. K, 54, XV cent. (1493), fol. 75 r; (6-7) Mentz (Munic. Lib., cod. 542, XIV-XV cent., fol. 85 r, and cod. 545, XV cent., fol. 196 r); (8) Rietberg (Lib. of Francis. Conv., cod. E, XV cent.); (9-10) Utrecht (Univ. Lib. cod. 173, XV cent., fol. 106 r, and cod. 174, XV cent., fol. 86 r); (11-12) Rome (archiv. of St. Isidore's College, MSS. 1/73 and 1/82). The two last named MSS. have their proper endings.

[107] For example, in class A, chap. xiii on Contemplation, and chap. xiv on the Active Life are found after chap. xii on Prayer; whereas in class B these two chapters are found united toward the end of the collection. So, too, in chap. ix, class B omits several "Sayings" on Chastity, but adds a chapter on Virtues, made up, as it seems, of "Sayings" found in other chapters. The differences between these two classes of MSS. are more marked toward the end where one contains "Sayings" not found in the other.

[108] This codex, which dates from about 1300, and which will be referred to as III, is to be found at the Laurentian Library (cod. 10, plut. XIX dextr. fol. 441v ff.), contains the title: "Ista sunt verba fratris Aegidii." The Prologue begins "Quia sermo Domini est vivus"; the collection itself begins "Cum nullus sit" and ends "in coelis dare promittit," followed by "explicunt verba fratris Aegidii." A similar collection, dating from the fifteenth century, is found at Munich (Royal Lib., cod. 11,354).

der. This codex may be said to represent a third collection.

IV. Yet a fourth collection of the "Dicta" may be found in MSS. which contain some "Sayings" of the first and all of the second collection, besides many others which are found in the Life of Blessed Giles, inserted in the "Chronica XXIV Generalium."[109]

So much for the early MS. collections of the "Dicta." Coming next to the printed editions, the first place among the Latin editions must be given to that printed by Peter Schöffer at Mentz in 1463.[110] A second Latin edition was issued at Cologne by Ulr. Zell about seven years later.[111] Others were published at Antwerp in 1534,[112] at Bologna in 1585,[113] at Sala-

[109] This third collection, which begins "Ut possis assequi quod intendis" and ends "sic mala consuetudo ad omne malum," shall hereafter be referred to as IV. It is found in two fourteenth century MSS. at Assisi (Munic. Lib. cod. 403, fol. 105 r, and cod. 676).

[110] "Verba aurea seu sententiae ad Christianam perfectionem aspirantibus utiles," Moguntiae, 1463, in 4. See Hurter: "Nom. Lit.," 2 ed., IV, 296.

[111] "Aurea verba S. Egidii ordinis Fratrum Minorum," Coloniae, Ulr. Zell, circa 1470. See "Biblioth. Hagiog. Latina," 16-17: 1308. See also Holthrop: "Catalogus Librorum Saeculo XV Impressorum" (Hague, 1856), P. 2da, p. 332, n. 69. (B. M., Univ. Lib., Cambridge, St. Genev., n. 1172.)

[112] "Sententiae vere aureae sancti Patris Aegidii Assismatis omnibus ad Christianam perfectionem aspirantibus utilissimae." Antverpia, MDXXXIV, apud Martinum Caeserem, in 8. See Hurter, l. c.

[113] This edition bears the same title as that of Antwerp.

manca in 1625,[114] at Brussels in 1655,[115] and elsewhere.[116]

Moreover, Bartholomew of Pisa [117] and the Bollandist Papebroche [118] have published collections of the " Dicta " in the " Liber de Conformitate " and the " Acta Sanctorum." [119] The selections contained in the works of St. Antoninus,[120] Surius,[121] Sedulius,[122] Rodolfo of Tossignano,[123] Wadding,[124] and others, hardly merit the name of a collection.

The " Dicta " have not only been edited in

[114] See Sbaralea "Supplementum" (Rome, 1806), p. 4.
[115] "Sententiae vere aureae sancti Patris Aegidii Assisiatis," Bruxellis, Foppens, MDCLV, in 32, p. 75 (copy in library of Friars Minor at Ghent). See "Etudes Franciscaines," t. xiv, n. 82, Oct. 1905.
[116] This list does not pretend to be complete. See Panzer: "Annales Typographici" (Nuremberg, 1797), vol. iv, p. 125, n. 464.
[117] See his " De Conformitate," (Ed. Milan, 1510), lib. I, fruct. viii, part 2. A critical edition of this work will form t. iv of the " Analecta Franciscana."
[118] See " Acta SS.," Aprilis iii, (Edit. 3a, 1866), pp. 228-238.
[119] The principal differences between the collections published in the " Liber de Conformitate " and the " Acta Sanctorum " is that the latter adds many additional " Sayings," namely, No. 54 to 62 ("ex solo MS. Antverpiensi"), etc.
[120] See " Chronicae," tit. xxiv, c. 8, § 12.
[121] See " Vitae SS." (1618), die 23 Aprilis.
[122] " Historia Seraphica " (Antwerp, 1613), pp. 97-98.
[123] See " Historiarum etc. libri tres " (Venice, 1586), pp. 63-66.
[124] See " Annales Minorum " (ed. 2da, Rome, 1732), t. iv, pp. 182-198.

Hermitage of the Carceri

Introduction lvii

Latin many times, but they have also been translated into different languages. An Italian version of the "Dicta" is found in many fifteenth-century MSS.[125] The first editions printed in Italian bear neither year nor place of publication, but clearly date from the fifteenth century. They are entitled: "Capitole di certa dottrina e detti notabili di frate Egidio terzo compagno di S. Francesco."[126] Some of these chapters which, if we may believe Zambrini,[127] were compiled or translated by Feo Belcari, one of the most celebrated Italian prose writers in the fourteenth century, were subsequently appended to certain editions of the "Fioretti"[128] and thus in course of time

[125] The version which begins "La grazia di Dio e le virtu" is contained principally in the following codices: (1) Donaueschingen (bibl. Fürstenberg, cod. 250, fol. 26); (2) Florence (National Lib., cod. 675, B, 2, fol. 227); (3) Seville (bibl. Columbina, cod. BB, 145, 11); (4) Ravenna (Munic. Lib., cod. 63, fol. 109); (5-6) Rome (Vatican Lib., cod. Vat. 9297, fol. 45 r, and cod. Ottob. 681, fol. 1 r); (7) Venice (St. Mark's Lib., cod. 61, cl. 1); (8) Vincenza (Bertolina Lib., cod. G, 2, 8, 18, fol. 71 r).

[126] See Panzer, op. cit., vol. iv, p. 78 n, and p. 125, n. 465; see also Hain: "Repertorium Bibliographicum" (1826-38), vol. i, p. 14, n. 104, and Hain-Copinger: "Sopplem." (1895-1902), pt. 1, p. 3, n. 105.

[127] Le opere volgari a stampa dei secoli XIII e XIV indicate e descritte, col. 409.

[128] This appendix is not found in any one of the sixteen editions of the "Fioretti" issued in the fifteenth century. But it finds a place in the epoch-making edition of Filippo Buonarroti (Florence, Tartini e Franchi, 1718), and in many subsequent ones.

passed into English,[129] French,[130] German,[131] and other languages, along with such translations of that ever delightful work as include the appendices.

German and Dutch translations of the "Dicta," dating from the fifteenth century, are extant in MS.[132] A complete German edition recently appeared,[133] besides an at-

[129] The first English translation of the "Fioretti," made more than forty years ago, under the auspices of Cardinal (then Monsignor) Manning, by the Marchesa di Salvo, Lady Georgiana Fullerton, and a Franciscan Sister of the Convent at Bayswater, contained such of the "Dicta" as form this appendix. (See "The Little Flowers of St. Francis," London, Burns and Lambart, 1864, pp. 219 ff.) This appendix finds no place in the translations of the "Fioretti" made by Abby Langdon Alger (Boston, Roberts Bros., 1887), or in that issued by the Franciscan Friars at Upton (reprinted 1899, London, Kegan Paul). There is, however, a translation of it published in pamphlet form by the London Catholic Truth Society and it has been retranslated by Prof. T. W. Arnold. See "The Little Flowers of St. Francis," London, Dent and Co., 1901, fifth edition, pp. 269 ff.

[130] "Petites Fleurs de S. François d'Assise," traduites de l'Italien pour la première fois par M. l'Abbé A. Riche, pretre de St. Sulpice. Sixième édit. (Montreal, 1901), p. 285 ff. See Bibliography, under "Œuvres."

[131] S. Franzisci Blumengartlein. Deutsch von Dr. Franz Kaulen, 2d ed. (Mayence, Kirchheim, 1880), p. 298 ff.

[132] There is a fifteenth-century German translation at Vienna, Bibl. Palat., cod. 13,880, fol. 288-310: and a Dutch translation of the same century at Leyden, Bibl. Acad., cod. 83.

[133] "Der Selige Aegidius von Assisi." Sein Leben und seine Sprüche. Von P. Gisbert Menge, O.F.M. Paderborn (Junfermann), 1906, in 12, pp. 118.

Introduction lix

tractive selection in Flemish.¹³⁴ To English readers, however, the "Dicta" have hitherto been inaccessible, except at secondhand, through extracts contained in the "Fioretti," and quotations given in other works. I am not unmindful that Sbaralea ¹³⁵ mentions an English translation of the "Dicta" as having been issued by Father Angelus a S. Francisco (Richard Mason), at Douai, in 1633; but diligent search has failed to reveal any trace of this work, or, indeed, any other reference to it. There is no mention of such a translation in the catalogue of the British Museum, nor is it found in the list of Father Angelus's works given by the historian of the second English Province of the Friars Minor.¹³⁶ So far as I have been able to ascertain, the "Dicta B. Aegidii" have never until now been presented in English. In any event, the recent revival of widespread interest in the early Franciscan literature is, perhaps, sufficient apology for

---

¹³⁴ "Sommeghe guldenen woerde seer stichtich die broeder Egidius ghesproeken heeft." In 't licht gegeven door Fr. Stephen Schoutens, O.F.M. Antwerp, De Wolf. 1904, in 4to, pp. 32, after the XV cent. MS. of Fr. Jan van Roest.

¹³⁵ See "Supplementum ad Scriptores trium ordinum S. Francisci" (Rome, 1806). A list of different editions of the "Dicta" is given on p. 4.

¹³⁶ See "The Franciscans in England, 1600-1850," by Father Thaddeus, O.F.M. (London: Art and Book Co. 1898), pp. 108-109.

offering a new and complete version of this work to English readers.

The ground was, so to say, cleared for the work of such a translation by the appearance last year, at Quaracchi, of a critical edition of the Latin text.[137] In this volume, which forms part of the " Bibliotheca Franciscana Ascetica Medii Aevi,"[138] we have for the first time a correct and critical Latin text of the " Dicta " printed after the collation with numerous codices. Indeed, in the preparation of this edition the " Patres Editores " of St. Bonaventure's College found themselves confronted by a sufficiently embarrassing number of MSS., not a few of which had suffered revision and addition: these they have classified as best they could.[139] They have accepted all

[137] " Dicta B. Aegidii Assisiensis," sec. codices MSS. emendata et denuo edita. Ad Claras Aquas (Quaracchi). 1905. In 16mo., pp. xx-124.

[138] The first volume in this series, comprising the "Opuscula S. P. Francisci," has also been translated into English by the present writer under the title of " The Writings of St. Francis of Assisi." Philadelphia, The Dolphin Press. 1906. Pp. xxxii-208.

[139] This work of collation was done largely by Father Gisbert Menge, O.F.M., now stationed at Paderborn, and who has recently published an excellent German translation of the " Dicta " (see above, p. lviii). The greater part of the MSS. in question are found in the " Collectaneis " of the lamented Father Fidelis of Fanna, O.F.M., preserved in the archives at St. Bonaventure's College, Quaracchi (see " Collection d'Etudes et de Documents," t. i, ii, and iv, and " Opuscules de critique historique," fasc. ii, v, and ix).

Introduction lxi

"Sayings" attributed to Giles in codices of the thirteenth and fourteenth centuries, basing their edition upon the second (II) of the MS. collections mentioned above [140] and following the order found in the compilation "Fac secundum exemplar." Sayings not found in both families of MSS. comprising this second collection form one Appendix; those not found in either form a second, while the Prologue is taken from the Florentine Codex of 1300. This arrangement, which makes for clearness and precludes unnecessary repetitions, has been adopted in the present translation. Throughout I have followed the reading of the Quaracchi text, but variants of any importance are indicated in footnotes.[141]

I should add that I have contributed the In-

---

[140] See p. liii.

[141] With few exceptions the differences between the texts of the various MSS. are unimportant, and a collation of them presents only minor difficulties. Where it has seemed that something might be gained by noting these variants and difficulties in a translation, I have done so. In such cases the following abbreviations have been used: —

Vat. — Vatican MS. 4354.
Is. — St. Isidore's MS. 1/63.
C — St. Isidore's MS. 1/73.
D — Laurentian MS. 10 plut. dextr. XIX.
E — Rietberg MS.
F — Assisi MS. 590.
G — Assisi MS. 121.
H — Oxford MS. 525.
Pis. — Version of Barth. of Pisa in the "Liber Conformitatum."
Ed. — Bollandist version in "Acta Sanctorum."

troduction, including the biographical sketch of Blessed Giles, which does not figure in the Quaracchi edition, the Bibliography, and Index, besides many original notes and references, the outcome of independent research work in Italy and elsewhere.

My chief aim, however, has been to translate the "Dicta" with a strict fidelity to the Latin which, let it be said parenthetically, is often far from classical, and not always easy to render. At least, in most instances Giles seems to have spoken in Italian, and in some passages those who took down his Sayings have simply Latinized the Italian; in others, the Latin words are used in an Italian sense. Here and there the Italian remains untranslated in the Latin text. Giles, because he was determined to be understood and because there was in him a strong strain of imagination, achieved a singularly clear and forcible manner of expressing the fundamental thoughts of his soul; but he was not always grammatically accurate: he spoke as one untrained to literary forms and he had not the scholar's range of words. Hence repetitions abound in his "Dicta." But since my desire has been to give as faithful an idea of Giles's own words as may be, I have not essayed to put any gloss upon such defects of a work in which it were foolish to look for literary style.

That I have not succeeded in doing justice to the original in the present translation I am but too well aware. However, I venture to hope that in spite of its shortcomings this effort to make "The Golden Sayings" of Blessed Giles better known to English readers, may be kindly received and may conduce to the same end as that which they had in view who first collected these "Sayings" in the far-off thirteenth century — the honor of God and the edification of those who read them.[142]

It only remains for me to record my sincere gratitude to Father Alessio Bracci of S. Maria degli Angeli for his kind help in securing illustrations; to Father Stephen Donovan for his careful revision of a large portion of the text; to Mr. Montgomery Carmichael for the loan of books and for many valuable suggestions, as well as to all others who have in any way assisted me in the preparation of this volume.

FR. PASCHAL ROBINSON, O.F.M.

Franciscan Convent,
Washington, D. C.
All Saints, 1906.

[142] See Prologue, p. 3.

GOLDEN SAYINGS OF
BLESSED BROTHER GILES

Aegidius, ut erat in Sanctarum Scripturarum lectione et meditatione assiduus, tantopere profecit ut omnia pene verba (ejus) gravida viderentur, quae comiter et quodam cum lepore saluberrima promere solebat, omniaque ipsius dicta argustissima quaedam apophthegmata dici possunt. —*Wadding:* "Scriptores Ordinis Minorum," p. 5.

Golden Sayings of Blessed Brother Giles

PROLOGUE

BECAUSE "the Word of God is living and effectual and more piercing than any two-edged sword": living by vivifying the dead; efficacious by giving medicine to the infirm, and more piercing than any two-edged sword in penetrating the hard of heart and reaching unto the division of soul and spirit[1] by separating vices from virtues, it seems meet and wholesome that the sayings of the servants of God, drawn not from human wisdom but with ineffable joy of heart from the fonts of the Saviour Jesus Christ, should be written down for the edification of posterity.

And therefore to the glory and honor of the Almighty God and the edification of our neighbors who may read or hear them, we have put down in writing most helpful to the soul the honeyed words which Brother Giles spoke from the fulness of his heart in holy conferences.

[1] See Heb. 4 : 12.

I

ON VIRTUES AND GRACES AND THEIR EFFECT, AND CONTRARIWISE OF VICES

THE graces of God and virtues are the ladder and way of ascending into heaven; but vices and sins are the way and the ladder of descending into hell.

Vices and sins are poison, and good works are the antidotes.

Grace draweth grace, and one vice leadeth to another vice.

Grace doth not seek to be praised, and vice doth not wish to be despised. That is, the man of grace doth not wish to be praised nor doth he seek human praise, and the man of vice doth not wish to be despised or reproved — which proceedeth from pride.

The mind findeth repose in humility: patience is its daughter.

Cleanness of heart seeth God: devotion assimilateth Him.

If thou lovest, thou shalt be loved; if thou fearest, thou shalt be feared; if thou servest, thou shalt be served; if thou behavest well toward others, others will behave well toward thee.

Blessed is he who loveth and doth not therefore desire to be loved; blessed is he who feareth and doth not therefore desire to be feared; blessed is he who serveth and doth not therefore desire to be served; blessed is he who behaveth well toward others and doth not desire that others behave well toward him; and because these are great things the foolish do not rise to them.

There are three things very great and useful which whosoever possesseth cannot fall into evil: the first is, if thou bearest in peace, for God's sake, all tribulation that may befall thee; the second is, if thou humblest thyself the more in all thou dost and receivest; the third is, if thou lovest faithfully those goods that cannot be seen with fleshly eyes.

Those things that are the more despised and neglected by worldly men are honored and valued by God and His saints, and those that are loved and caressed and honored the more by worldly men are still more hated and abandoned and despised by God and His saints. Man hateth all that should be loved and loveth all that should be hated.

Brother Giles once asked a certain Brother, saying: "Is it well with thy soul?" He replied: "My Brother, I know not." Brother Giles said: "Holy contrition, holy humility, holy charity, holy devotion, and holy joy make the soul holy and good."

II

ON FAITH AND ON THE INCOMPREHENSIBILITY OF GOD

ALL that can be thought of, seen, told, and touched, is nothing in respect to what can neither be thought of, told, seen, nor touched.

All the wise and holy men who have been, are, and will be, who have spoken or will speak of God, have not spoken nor will they ever speak of God in comparison to what He is, save as the prick of a needle is in comparison to heaven and earth and to all the creatures that are in them, and more than a thousand times less. For all Holy Scripture speaketh to us, as it were lispingly, even as a mother lispeth with her little son because otherwise he could not understand her words.[1]

Brother Giles once said to a certain secular Judge:[2] "Believest thou that the gifts of God are great?" The Judge answered: "I believe." Brother Giles said to him: "I will show thee

---

[1] See "Chron. XXIV General.," p. 109, for Giles's interview with the two Dominicans in which he illustrates this truth more strikingly.

[2] The Latin reads: "Judex saecularis."

that thou believest not," and he added: "How much are all thy possessions worth?" The Judge replied: "They are worth, perhaps, a thousand pounds."[3] Brother Giles said to him: "Wouldst thou give them for ten thousand pounds?" He replied: "I would give them very willingly." Brother Giles said to him: "It is certain that all earthly things are nothing with respect to heavenly things; why then dost thou not give those for these?" The Judge answered: "Believest thou that any man doth as much as he believeth?" Brother Giles answered: "Holy men and women have striven to put in practice the good things they believed and were able to do, and what they could not carry out in deed they supplied by holy desires; the holy desire made up for the defect in the work. If any one should have perfect faith, he would come to a state in which the fulness of certitude would be vouchsafed him. If, therefore, thou believest, thou workest aright."[4]

The man who with certitude awaiteth the great and eternal good — what harm can any evil do him? and the man who awaiteth the great and eternal evil — what benefit can any good be to him? A man who hath lost the

---

[3] The Latin reads " mille libras."
[4] See "Chron. XXIV General.," p. 94. Codex C adds, "The Judge acquiesced and declared Brother Giles's opinion to be true."

good of all goods — what good can the angels and all the saints of heaven restore to him? How can he be consoled, and who can console him? No one save the Divine visitation.

Withal a sinner ought never to despair of the mercy of God while he liveth; for there is hardly a tree so thorny and gnarled that men may not make it smooth and pretty and ornament it. So much the more there is no sinner in the world so great whom God cannot in many ways adorn with grace and virtues.

The Grotto of Blessed Brother Giles at the Carceri
(The Friar seen in the picture is standing at the right of the entrance)

III

ON LOVE

LOVE is greater than all other virtues. Blessed is he who is not satiated with those things which he ought always to desire.

Brother Giles said to a certain Brother, his spiritual friend, "Believest thou that I love thee?" This Brother answered, "I believe." Brother Giles said to him: "Believe not that I love thee, for the Creator alone is the one who truly loveth the creature: and the love of the creature is nothing in respect to the love of the Creator."

And a certain other Brother said: "Brother Giles, what is it that the prophet saith: 'Every friend will walk deceitfully'?"[1] To whom Brother Giles answered: "Therefore am I deceitful to thee because I make not thy good mine own, for the more I were to make thy good mine, so much the less would I be deceitful to thee. And the more one shall rejoice at the good of a neighbor, so much the more shall he in consequence be partaker thereof. If then thou wilt be partaker in the good of

---

[1] Jerem. 9:4.

all, rejoice in the good of all. Hence, make the good of others thine own, if it pleaseth thee: and make the evil of others thy care, if it displeaseth thee. This is the way of salvation, that thou rejoicest in the good of a neighbor and grievest in his evil, and thinkest good of others and evil of thyself, and honorest others and despisest thyself.

He who doth not wish to honor others shall not be honored, and he who doth not wish to know shall not be known, and he who doth not wish to bear fatigue shall not rest.

To cultivate piety and kindness is a work fruitful above every other work.

Whatever is without love and benevolence is not pleasing to God and His Saints.

By his own works a man is made poor, and by divine works he is made rich: hence a man must love divine things and despise his own.

What is greater than to know how to commend the benefits of God and to know how to reprove oneself for one's own wrongdoings? In this school, namely in the pondering and commending the benefits of God and in pondering and blaming my own wrongdoings, I would wish to have studied from the beginning of the world, if I only had lived, and to study to the end of the world, if I were going to live; and if I were wanting in reproving myself for my own wrongdoings, I would not wish to be wanting in the considering of the benefits of God.

Thou seest that mimics and jongleurs [2] in a wonderful way commend those who give them a piece of clothing: [3] what, therefore, ought we to do to the Lord our God?

Thou oughtest to be faithful in the love of Him who desireth to free thee from every evil and who desireth to give thee every good.

[2] Reference to this class of Provençal minstrels, who, later on, degenerated into mere buffoons, is frequent in the early Franciscan literature. St. Francis wished his Friars to be the Lord's Minstrels. (See "Spec. Perf.," ed. Sabatier, cap. 100.) And in Celano's account of St. Clare's death, Brother Juniper is referred to as "the eminent Minstrel of the Lord." (See "Acta SS.," Aug. II, p. 764.)

[3] Ed. reads "a little gift."

IV

ON HOLY HUMILITY

NO one can come to the knowledge of God except through humility.

The way of going above is to go below.

All the perils and all the great disasters that have taken place in the world would not have happened save for holding the head high, as is clear in the case of him who was created in heaven, and of Adam, and of the pharisee in the Gospel, and many others. And all the great good that has taken place has been on account of inclining the head, as is clear in the case of the Blessed Virgin, of the publican, of the good thief, and of many others.

Blessed Giles also said: "O! that we might have a great pack which would always make us bend our head!"

A certain Brother said to him: "How can we flee from this pride?" And he said: "For this wash thy hands and there put thy mouth where thou keepest thy feet.[1] If thou wert to consider the benefits of God, thou oughtest to

---

[1] Codex Vat. reads: "for this lift thy hands." Codices Is., C, and D: "for this wash thy hands unless thou place"; F and G: "where thou placest thy mouth."

bow thy head; and if thou wert to consider thy sins, thou oughtest to bow thy head in like manner. Woe to him who wisheth to be honored on account of his badness."

A great degree of humility in man is to know that he is always opposed to his own welfare. I consider it also the fruit of humility for one to give up what doth not belong to him and not to appropriate it to oneself—that is, to attribute all good things to God to whom they belong and evil things to oneself.

Blessed is he who esteemeth himself as vile before man, as he knoweth himself to be vile in the sight of God.

Blessed is he who judgeth himself now, for he will not come to another judgment.

Blessed is he who walketh faithfully according to the judgment and obedience of another, for this the Apostles did even after they had been filled with the Holy Ghost.

He who wisheth to have peace and quiet should esteem every man his superior.

Blessed is he who doth not want to appear in his words and manner save in that way in which Divine Grace hath fashioned him.

Blessed is he who knoweth how to keep and hide the revelations of God, for there is nothing hidden which God may not reveal when it pleaseth Him.

If a man were to be holier than any in the world and were to reckon himself more contemptible than any in the world — in this would there be humility.

Humility knoweth not how to speak, and patience dareth not speak.

Humility seemeth to me to be like lightning: for as lightning causeth terrible flashes and nothing can afterward be found of it, thus humility dissipateth every evil and is the foe of every sin and causeth man to esteem himself as nothing.

Through humility man findeth grace before God and peace with men. For, as a great king, if he wished to send his daughter to some place, would not put her on an unmanageable, proud, and kicking horse, but upon a gentle and easy-going horse — just so the Lord doth not place His grace in the proud but in the humble.

V

ON THE HOLY FEAR OF THE LORD

THE holy fear of the Lord expelleth all evil fear and guardeth those good things which cannot be told in words or even thought of: it is not given to all to have this fear, because it is a very great gift.

He that feareth not, showeth that he hath nothing to lose.

The fear of God ruleth and governeth man and bringeth him into the grace of God; which, if a man possesseth, the fear of the Lord preserveth it; and if he hath it not, it leadeth him to it. All rational creatures that have fallen would never have fallen had they possessed this gift. This holy gift belongeth not save to holy men and women; and howsoever much any one be full of grace, he is none the less humble and timorous, and the virtue that is least practised by men is not less than the others.

A man that hath so far offended his God that he is worthy of death — with what security can he go into the presence of God?

Blessed is he who knoweth for a truth that

in this world he is in a prison and that he hath always offended his God.

A man oughteth to be very much afraid of his pride lest it hurl him down.

Ever fear and beware of thyself and of him that is like unto thee.

There is no perfect safety for a man whilst he is in the midst of his enemies.

Our enemy is our flesh and along with the demons it is ever opposed and contrary to the soul: hence man oughteth to have a greater fear of himself than of anything else in the world, lest his own malice vanquish him. It is impossible for man to ascend to the grace of God or to persevere in it, without holy fear and holy dread. He that hath it not, possesseth a portent that he will perish.

This fear maketh one obey humbly and bow the head to the earth under the yoke of obedience.

Even so the greater fear one possesseth, so much the more doth he pray: but no small thing is his to whom the grace of holy prayer is given.

The works of man, however great they may seem, are not according to the estimation of man but according to the estimation and good pleasure of God. And hence[1] it behoveth us to fear always.

[1] Ed. reads: "And 'first' it behoveth," etc.

VI

ON PATIENCE

HE that would bear tribulations patiently for God's sake would quickly attain to great grace: he would be lord of this world and would have one foot already in the other world.

Whatever a man doth, whether good or evil, he doth it unto himself: thou oughtest not therefore to be scandalized if any one do thee harm, but thou oughtest to have compassion because of his sin.

Bear patiently the injuries done thee by thy neighbor for God's sake, for thy neighbor's sake, and for thine own sake.

In so far as one is ready to bear tribulations and injuries for God's sake, so great is he before God and not more; and in so far as one is cowardly in bearing tribulations and sorrows for God's sake, so much the less is he before God and he doth not know what God is.

If some one speaketh ill to thee, help him; if some one speaketh well to thee, refer it to God: thou oughtest however to help him, so that if he speaketh ill to thee thou mayest speak worse of thyself.

If thou wouldst do thy part well, do thy part ill and the part of another well: that is, praise the deed and word of another and reprove thine own; and if thou wouldst do thy part ill, do the contrary. When therefore any one contendeth with thee, lose if thou wouldst win: for in the end when thou thinkest to have won, thou wilt find that thou hast lost. The way of loss is therefore the way of salvation.

We are not good bearers of tribulation, because we are not good seekers after spiritual consolations: for he who would labor faithfully in himself and above himself and for himself would bear all things sweetly.

Do injury to no one; and if any one do injury to thee, bear it patiently for the love of God and the remission of thy sins. For it is much better to bear one grievous wrong for the love of God without any murmuring than to feed one hundred paupers for many days and to fast daily for many days even till the heavens are starry.[1] What doth it profit a man to despise himself and to afflict his body in fasts and prayers and watchings and disciplines, and not to be able to bear one injury from his neighbor by reason of which he

---

[1] Ed. adds in note, "that is, until night time when the stars may be seen in the sky."

would receive a far greater reward than for those things which he sustaineth of his own accord: and this is the reason why insult offered trieth latent pride.

To bear tribulations without murmur purifieth the sins of men more than the shedding of tears.

Blessed is he who ever keepeth before his eyes his own sin and the benefits of God, and who patiently beareth every trial and tribulation, for he hath reason to hope for great consolation.

Blessed is he who doth not ask or desire any consolation under heaven from any creature.

A man ought not to expect a reward from God if he is humble and quiet, only whilst he is well satisfied in all things.

He that keepeth his sins ever well before his eyes shall not give way in any trial.

Every good which thou hast thou oughtest to receive from God and every evil from thy sin, for if one man had done and were to do all the good that all men in the world have done, are doing, and will do yet, if he were to look well into himself, he would find himself ever contrary to his own welfare.

A certain Brother said to him: "What shall we do, if great tribulations should come in our time?" Brother Giles answered: "If the Lord should rain stones and rocks from heaven they would not harm us, if we were such as we ought to be. If man were such as he ought to be, evil would for him be turned to good. For just as in one having a bad will, good itself is distorted into evil, even so in one having a good will, evil is changed into good. For all great goods and the great evils are from within man and cannot be seen."

The worst demons run after great infirmity and great labor and great hunger and at great wrongs done to any one.

If thou wouldst be saved, ask not that justice be done to thee by any creature.[2]

Holy men do good and suffer evil.

If thou knowest that thou hast offended the Lord thy God, the Creator and Lord of all things, know that it is meet that all should persecute thee and avenge the injury thou hast done to thy Lord.

Thou oughtest to bear patiently injuries and wrongs done to thee by all creatures, because thou hast not justice against any one since thou art worthy to be punished by all.

It is a great virtue for a man to overcome himself. If thou overcomest thyself, thou overcomest all thine enemies and attainest to every good.

It is a great virtue if one suffereth himself to be overcome by men, for such a man is the lord of this world.

[2] See St. Bonav. "Epist. XXV Memorial.," n. 5 (Opera Omnia, t. viii, p. 493).

If thou wouldst be saved, strive to be without hope of all consolation that any mortal creature can give thee, because the falls which occur from consolation are greater and more frequent than those arising from tribulation.

Noble is the nature of the horse which, though it be going at the most rapid pace, yet he that rideth can turn it from one way and direct it toward another: thus ought man in the vehemence of his wrath suffer himself to be ruled by the one that correcteth him.

At the mere memory of God a man ought to wish — in so far as he is concerned — to pay a price to others in order that they should give him slaps and buffets and drag him by the hair.

A certain religious once murmured in his presence on account of some difficult command given him. The holy Brother Giles said to him: "My friend, the more thou murmurest, so much the more dost thou burden thyself; and the more thou devoutly and humbly bowest thy head beneath the yoke of holy obedience, so much the lighter and sweeter will it be to thee. Thou wilt not be reviled in this world, and wilt thou be honored in another? Thou wilt not be cursed, and wilt thou be blessed? Thou wilt not labor, and wilt thou rest? Thou art deceived, for through revilement we come to honor, through malediction blessing is obtained, and through work rest. The proverb is true: He that doth not give of that which he regretteth [3] cannot have of that which he desireth. Wonder not if thy neighbor sometimes offendeth thee, for even Martha who was holy wished to stir up the Lord against her own sister Mary. But Martha murmured against Mary unjustly, for the more Mary had lost the use of her members than Martha, so much the more did she labor than Martha, for she had lost speech, sight, hearing, taste, and movement. Try to be affable and virtuous and fight against vices and bear tribulations and shames with patience. For there is nothing else save that thou overcome thyself, because it is little for a man to draw souls to God unless he overcometh himself."

[3] Codex G for "regretteth" reads "desireth," and Ed. "oughteth."

VII

ON HOLY SOLICITUDE AND WATCHFULNESS OF HEART[1]

THE slothful man[2] loseth this world and the other, bringing forth no fruit for himself or for others.

It is impossible for virtues to be acquired without solicitude and toil.

If thou canst be in certainty, place not thyself in doubt: he is in certainty who laboreth for God and for the eternal kingdom.

The youth who refuseth to labor, rejecteth the kingdom of heaven.

If solicitude doth not avail, negligence doth not hinder or hurt: because if good doth not profit, evil doth not harm.

As unholy sloth is the way of going to hell, even so idleness and holy quiet is the way of going to heaven.

A man oughteth to be very careful to preserve the grace given him by God and to labor faithfully with it, for man often loseth fruit for leaves and grain for straws.

[1] In Pis. this chapter is entitled " On Slothfulness."
[2] Ed. reads " religious."

To some the Lord giveth fruit and leaveth them in want of leaves, to some, however, He giveth both, and some lack both.

I consider it greater to preserve the good things given by the Lord than to acquire them. He who knoweth how to acquire and knoweth not how to store up will never become rich, but to know how to store up and not to know how to acquire is not a great thing.

Many acquire much but never become rich, because they do not guard what they have gained; and others gain little by little and become rich, for that which they gain they guard well.

What a mass of water the river Tiber would hold if it were not continually flowing!

Man asketh from God a gift without measure and without end, and he wisheth to serve Him with measure and with end. Whoever therefore wisheth to be loved and rewarded without end, oughteth to serve and love without end and without measure.

Man loseth his perfection because of his negligence.

The holy Brother Giles once spoke to a certain person wishing to go to Rome, saying: "When thou art on the way do not draw toward thee those things which thou shalt see, lest they hinder thee; and learn to detect good money from false: for many are the artifices of the enemy and his snares are various and hidden." [3]

Blessed is he who employeth his body for love of the Most High, and for the good which he doth he shall not require any reward short of that from heaven.[4]

If a man were exceeding poor and some one should say to him: Brother, I will lend thee this thing of mine that for three days thou mayst trade with it and for this thou shalt receive an infinite treasure; would not this poor man, if it were evident to him that this were true, strive diligently to trade with that thing? The thing lent to us by God is our flesh, and three days are as it were the whole time of our life: if then thou wouldst have enjoyment, strive to gain: for if thou toilest not, how shalt thou rest?

If all the fields and vineyards of this world belonged to one man who did not cultivate them or cause them to be cultivated, what fruit would he derive therefrom? But another having a small portion of fields and vineyards and cultivating them well, deriveth therefrom fruit for himself and for many others.

If a man wisheth to do wrong, he hardly asketh advice; and when he wisheth to do good, he seeketh to obtain counsel from many.

[3] See "Chron. XXIV General.," p. 107, and Pis. c. i.
[4] Ed. reads: "Of the good which is in heaven."

It is a common [5] proverb: Do not put the pot on the fire counting upon thy neighbor [6] (to fill it).

A man is not blessed if he hath a good will, unless he striveth to follow it up with good works; for it is to this end that God giveth His grace to man — that he may follow it up.

A certain man who, as it seems, was a vagabond, once said to the holy Brother Giles: "Brother Giles, give me consolation." [7] Brother Giles replied: "Strive to behave well, and thou shalt have consolation."

Unless a man prepareth a place for God within himself, he shall never find place among the creatures of God.

Who is he that is not willing to do what would be best in this world not only for his soul but also for his body? But we desire to work neither the good of the soul nor the body.

I could swear of a truth that he who would lighten the yoke of the Lord for himself, maketh it the heavier; and he who burdeneth himself the more, maketh it the lighter.

---

[5] F. and G. read: "ironical."
[6] Is. for neighbor reads: "enemy."
[7] The word "consolatio" in medieval Latin has more than one meaning, as in modern Italian: "far consolazione" may signify "to eat." In the present case "fac mihi consolationem" is equivalent to asking an alms. See Du Cange: "Glossar. med. et inf. Latinit," s. v. Consolatio.

O! that all men might do that which would be best even for their body in this world!

He who hath made another world hath made this, and He is able to bestow in this of the goods which He bestoweth in another world; and the body shareth in the goods of the soul, for the good and evil of the soul extend to its body.

Then a certain Brother said to him: "Perhaps we shall die before we know our own good and experience any good." Brother Giles answered: "Tanners know about skins, cobblers about shoes, smiths about iron, and so on in the other trades: for how can a man know a trade in which he hath not practised? Thinkest thou that mighty lords give great gifts to foolish men and lunatics? They do not."

As good works are the way to all good, even so evil works are the way to all evil.

Blessed is he whom no thing under heaven shall disedify, and whom all things which he shall see or hear or know shall edify, and who shall seek to turn all things to his own utility.

VIII

ON CONTEMPT OF THE WORLD

WOE to that man who placeth his heart and desire and his strength in earthly things, on account of which he abandoneth and loseth heavenly and eternal good.

The eagle which flieth very high would not fly so high if it had one of the beams of St. Peter's Church tied to each wing.

I find many toiling for the body and few for the soul, for many toil for the body by breaking rocks, razing mountains, and performing other works fatiguing to the body, but who is there that laboreth so courageously and fervently for his soul?

The avaricious man is like a mole which doth not believe there is any other treasure or any other good except to burrow in the earth and to dwell in it; yet there are other treasures of which it is ignorant.

The birds of the air and the beasts of the earth and the fish of the sea are content when they have sufficient food for themselves; since therefore man is not content with earthly things but always sigheth after others, it is clear that he was not made chiefly for those but for the other. For the body was made for the sake of the soul and this world for the sake of the other world.

This world is a field of such a kind that he who hath the greater part of it hath the worst part.

He also used to say that the ants were not very pleasing to the Blessed Francis, because of their exceeding solicitude in collecting their food; but the birds of the air were most pleasing to him, since they "do not gather into barns." [1]

[1] Matt. 6 : 26.

IX

ON HOLY CHASTITY

OUR flesh is like the swine which eagerly runneth to the mud and delighteth to be in the mire.

Our flesh is like the tumble-bug which always delighteth to wallow in horse dung.

Our flesh is the devil's champion.

Our flesh is the devil's woodland.

The devil doth not despair of a man so long as he seeth him to have flesh.

A man having a borrowed animal maketh as much use of it as he can; even so ought we to do with the flesh.

It is impossible for man to attain to grace unless he divest himself of his fleshliness.

Although a man owning a beast may burden it in bearing heavy loads, and although he may feed it well withal, it will not go along the road aright without the rod of correction: so it is with the body of the penitent.

A certain Brother said to him: "How may we guard against the vices of the flesh?"[1]

---

[1] See "Chron. XXIV General.," p. 89, for an interesting discussion on this head between Giles, Rufinus, Juniper, and Simon, in which Giles sides with Juniper.

The holy Brother Giles answered him: "He that would move a great rock or large beams studieth how to move them more by skill than by strength, and in this case we must proceed in like manner."

Every vice woundeth chastity; for chastity is like a clear mirror which is obscured by a mere breath.

It is impossible for a man to arrive at the grace of God so long as it pleaseth him to delight in fleshly things. Turn, therefore, and return, above and below, on one side and on the other, there remaineth nothing save to fight against the flesh which seeketh to betray thee day and night: he that vanquisheth it vanquisheth all his foes and attaineth to every good.

But he used to say: "Among all the virtues I prefer holy chastity."

A certain Brother said to him: "Is not charity a greater virtue than chastity?" To whom Brother Giles replied: "And what is more chaste than charity?" And often he would say, singing: "O holy chastity, of what sort art thou, of what sort art thou? Thou art of such sort and so great that the foolish know not what thou art and how great."

A certain Brother said to him: "What dost thou mean by chastity?" Brother Giles answered: "By chastity I mean to keep custody of all the senses by the grace of God."[2]

---

[2] Codex F puts what follows in chap. xxiii.

On one occasion, whilst Brother Giles was commending chastity greatly, a certain married man approached him, saying: "I keep away from all women except my own wife: is it enough for me to do this?" Who answered: "Doth it not seem to thee that a man can get drunk on the wine of his own goblet?" Who said: "He can." And the holy Brother Giles said: "So it is in the present case."

Another person said to him: "Brother Giles, the Apostle doth not seem to speak save of a widowed woman 'who living in pleasures is dead.'"[3] Brother Giles answered him: "Although this word may be said of widows, yet this word applieth wherever it is applicable."

And the holy Giles said to the bystanders: "Where many thorns and other like things have sprung up in the ground which has long stood untilled and is now almost growing wild — in it is digging a great labor. Even so it is with the miserable sinner who remaineth long in sin and is full of vices: it is necessary to work much with him in preaching and in persuading before thou canst lead him in the way of salvation and unto fruitful works."

Then he spoke, saying: "See, O man, what thou lovest and for what thou lovest — heaven or earth, the Creator or the creature, light or darkness, the carnal or the spiritual, good or

[3] See 1 Tim. 5:6.

evil, and afterward thou shalt be the better able to separate good from bad and to see what things are to be loved and what to be hated." [4]

[4] Many of the "Sayings" in this chapter are contained in the " Chron. XXIV General.," p. 88. Pis. ends: "like a clear mirror" as is said above. Ed. places some of these " Sayings " elsewhere. (No. 75.)

X

ON THE COMBAT WITH TEMPTATIONS

GREAT grace cannot be possessed in peace because many wars always arise against it. For the more a man is in a state of grace so much the more is he attacked by the devil. But man ought not on that account to cease to follow up his grace, because the harder the fight so much the greater, if he prevaileth, will be the crown.

If we have not[1] many hindrances it is because we are not such as we ought to be. Yet if one were to walk well in the way of the Lord, we would suffer neither fatigue nor tediousness, but in the way of the world man suffereth fatigue and tedium until death.

A certain Brother answering him, said: "Thou seemest to say two things, one contrary to the other." The holy Brother Giles replied: "Do not the demons run after a man of good will rather than after others? Behold the hindrance! And if one should sell his small wares for a thousand times more than

[1] Ed. omits "not."

their value, what weariness would he then feel? Behold, the contradiction is solved! I say, therefore, that the more one is full of virtues so much the more is he pursued by vices, and so much the more ought he to hate them. By every vice thou conquerest thou acquirest virtue, and by whatever vice thou art troubled most from that thou shalt receive the greater crown if thou conquerest."

For whatsoever reason a man neglecteth to walk by the way of God, he for that very reason loseth his reward.

A certain person said to him: "I am frequently tempted with a most grievous temptation, and I have often asked God that he would take it away from me, and He doth not take it away." The holy Brother Giles replied to him: "The better any king armeth his soldiers with armor, the more he wisheth that they should fight valiantly."[2]

And a certain Brother then asked him, saying: "What may I do that I may go to prayer willingly when I feel dry and indevout?" Who answering, said: "Behold a certain king who hath two servants, of whom one is armed, but the other is unarmed; and these have to go to war. The one that is armed proceedeth valiantly to battle, but the other one unarmed thus addresseth his lord: 'My lord, as thou seest, I have no arms; but for love of thee

[2] See "Chron. XXIV General.," p. 93.

I go forth to the battle even without arms.' The king, however, seeing the faithfulness of the servant saith to his attendants: 'Go, prepare arms with which this my faithful servant may be adorned, and place on him the seal of my arms.'³ So, too, if any one goeth to the battle of prayer as if without arms, because he feeleth himself dry and indevout, God, seeing his fidelity, placeth on him the seal of his arms.⁴

"Even so is it with temptations, as it happeneth to a farmer who seeth a forest of trees and of brier bushes in a certain piece of his land in which he desireth to till afresh,⁵ and sow with grain, but he is worn out by many labors and sweatings and troubles before he can gather grain thence, and at times he almost repenteth that he hath undertaken the task because of the toil and the difficulties that beset him in the work. For first he beholdeth the woodland that must be cleared of trees, and then he seeth not the grain; secondly, he cutteth down the trees with much toil and pulleth up the roots of the trees, and he seeth not the grain;⁶ thirdly, he breaketh up and pre-

---

³ F, G, and Pis. omit all of this paragraph up to the words: "So too if any one," etc. Ed. omits from the words "the better any king" in the preceding paragraph to "even so is it with temptations" in the following.

⁴ See "Chron. XXIV General.," p. 93.

⁵ The Latin reads: "in quo vellet facere novale."

⁶ Pis., F, G, and Ed.: "he cutteth down the trees and

pareth the ground, and seeth not there the grain for which he hath labored so much; fourthly, he ploweth the ground again; fifthly, he soweth the grain; sixthly, he weedeth it; seventhly, he reapeth it; eighthly, he thresheth it; and all these things he doth with much labor; ninthly, he storeth it with joy as if unmindful of so much toil because of the quantity of fruit which he obtaineth thence in the end; many other labors besides these doth he sustain, all of which he blesseth because of joy that he seeth good fruit."

A certain person again said to him: "What can I do — for if I do anything good I am therefore filled with vainglory, and if I do evil I fall into sadness and wellnigh into despair?" The holy Brother Giles replied: "Thou dost well if thou grievest because of thy sin. However, I counsel thee that thou grieve moderately; for thou oughtest always to believe that the power of God is greater in forgiving than thy power in sinning. If God showeth mercy to some great sinner, believest thou that He abandoneth a lesser sinner? For the rest, desist not from doing good because of the temptation of empty glory. For if the farmer wishing to strew seed upon the ground should say within himself: 'I do not wish to sow this year, for if I shall have sown, perhaps the birds

seeth not yet the grain; thirdly, with much and grievous labor he pulleth up the roots."

will come and eat of that seed,' and for this reason he should not sow, he would have nothing to eat of the fruits of the earth; if, however, he soweth, even though some of the seed perisheth, yet the greater part will remain to him. So it is with him who is tempted by vainglory and fighteth against it." [7]

A certain Brother said to Brother Giles: "It is related of Blessed Bernard that he once said the seven penitential psalms, and that he did not think of anything else except of the things which he was saying." The holy Brother Giles answered: "I esteem it greater if some camp should be attacked violently and the sentinel of the camp defendeth himself bravely and manfully."

[7] See "Chron. XXIV General.," p. 94.

XI

ON PENANCE[1]

A CERTAIN secular Judge once said: "Brother Giles, how can we seculars ascend to the state of grace and virtue?" To whom Brother Giles answered: "A man must first be sorry for his sins, then confess uprightly, then perform humbly the penance imposed upon him, afterward keep himself from all sin and every occasion of sin; finally, he ought to exercise himself in good works."

Blessed is that evil which is turned for man into good, and cursed is that good which is turned for man into evil.

A man ought willingly to bear evil in this world because in this our Lord Jesus Christ gave us an example in Himself.

Blessed is he who shall have sorrow for his sins, and shall weep night and day, and shall not be consoled in this world until he cometh thither where all the desires of his heart shall be fulfilled.

---

[1] For Brother Gratian's testimony to Giles's own penitential practices see "Chron. XXIV General.," p. 88.

XII

ON PRAYER AND ITS EFFECT

PRAYER is the beginning and the end of all good. Prayer illumineth the soul, and by it all good and evil is known.

This prayer every sinner should offer to the Lord — that He may give him to know his own misery and his sins, and His benefits.

He who knoweth not how to pray doth not know God.

All who would be saved, if they have the use of reason, must of necessity give themselves up to prayer in their last end.

Let us suppose that a certain woman, very simple and shy, had an only son, dearly beloved, who, because of some crime, was taken prisoner by the king and led to the gallows, would not this woman, although shy and simple, cry out aloud, with dishevelled hair, and with bared breast, and run to the king, asking for the liberation of her son? Who, I ask, taught that simple soul to petition for her son? Was it not the love of her son and necessity that both made this shy woman, who hardly ever went beyond the threshold of her house,

Monteripido

almost audacious, running abroad among men on the streets, and that made her who was simple, wise? Even so he would desire and know how to pray well who fully realized his own evils and dangers and losses.

A certain Brother said to him: "A man should grieve much when he cannot find the grace of devotion in prayer." Brother Giles replied: "I counsel thee to proceed slowly, for if thou hadst a little wine in a goblet and there were some dregs under the wine, would'st thou wish to shake the goblet and mix the wine with the dregs? This is not to be done. And if the grindstone of a mill at times doth not make good flour, the miller doth not thereupon smash it with a hammer, but slowly and by degrees he mendeth that stone, and it afterward grindeth good flour. Do thou in like manner, and consider that thou art in no wise worthy to receive any consolation from God in prayer, for if a person had lived from the beginning of the world until now, and were to live to the end of the world, and each day at prayer his eyes gave forth a dishful of tears, he would not be worthy even at the end of the world that God should give him even one single consolation." [1]

A certain Brother once said to him: "Why doth a man suffer more temptations when he prayeth to God than at other times?" to

---

[1] See "Chron. XXIV General.," p. 87.

whom the holy Brother Giles answered: "When any one hath a lawsuit against an adversary in the court of any prince, if that man goeth to the prince in order to propose that something be done against his adversary, the latter on hearing this opposeth him with all his might lest the decision be given against him; even so the devil proceedeth against us. Hence if thou art engaged in conversation with others thou wilt notice often that thou dost not experience many attacks of temptation; but if thou shalt have gone to prayer to refresh thy soul thou shalt feel the fiery arrows of the enemy against thee. Thou oughtest not, however, for this reason to leave off prayer but stand firm, for this is the way to the supernal country; and he who on this account abandoneth prayer is as the one who fleeth from battle."

A certain person said to him: "I see many who seem to have the grace of devotion and of tears as soon as they go to pray. I, however, can scarce feel anything from it." Brother Giles answered: "Labor faithfully and devoutly, for the grace which God doth not give thee at one time He may give thee at another time, and what He doth not give thee in one day, in one week, or in one month, or in one year, He is able to give thee in another day, or in another week, or in another month or year. Place thy labor humbly in

Of Brother Giles 43

the Lord, and God will place His grace in thee as it may be pleasing to Him. A workman who maketh a knife striketh many blows upon the metal from which he maketh the knife before the knife is finished, but in the end the knife is finished with one blow." [2]

A man ought to be very solicitous as to his salvation, for if the whole world were full of men even up to the clouds, if that were possible, and among all these none was to be saved but only one, yet each should follow up his grace so that he might be that one, for to lose heaven is not to lose a shoe-latchet. But woe betide us! There is one who giveth and there is none who receiveth.

At another time a certain Brother asked the holy Brother Giles: "What dost thou, Brother Giles?" He replied: "I do evil." But the former again said to Brother Giles: "What evil dost thou who art a Friar Minor?" And Brother Giles said to a certain Friar Minor standing by: "Brother, who is the more ready: God to give His grace, or we to receive it?" The Brother replied: "God is more ready to give to us than we are to accept." The holy Brother Giles said to him: "And do we do well?" The Brother answered: "Indeed we do ill." And Brother Giles, turning to him who had questioned him as to what he was doing, said: "Behold, it is plain that

[2] See "Chron. XXIV General.," p. 78.

I spoke truly to thee when I replied that I was doing evil."

He likewise said: "Many works are commended in Holy Scripture, such as to clothe the naked, feed the hungry, and so forth,[3] but the Lord speaking of prayer, saith: 'For the Father seeketh such to adore Him.'[4] Good works adorn the soul, but prayer is something exceeding great."

Holy religious are like wolves which rarely go abroad, except for a great necessity, and then they tarry but a short while in public.

A certain Brother who was familiar with Brother Giles said to him: "Why dost thou not go forth sometimes to secular men wishing to speak to thee?"[5] Brother Giles, answering, said: "I wish to do good to my neighbor with profit to my soul. Believest thou not that I would rather at once give a thousand pounds[6] if I had them than give myself to my neighbor?" The Brother replied: "I believe." Brother Giles said: "And believest thou that I would rather give four thousand pounds[7] than give myself once to my neighbor?" The Brother replied: "I believe." Brother Giles

---

[3] E.g. Is. 58:7, and Matt. 25:35 ff.
[4] See John 4:23.
[5] The Brother in question seems to have been none other than Bernard of Quintavalle. See "Chron. XXIV General.," p. 110.
[6] Is. reads "marchas."
[7] Is. reads ten thousand "marchas."

said to him: "The Lord saith in the Gospel, 'whosoever hath left father and mother and brother and sister, etc., for My Name's sake shall receive an hundredfold in this world.'[8] But there was a certain Roman who entered the Order of Friars Minor whose goods were said to be valued at sixty thousand pounds; hence it is something great that the Lord God giveth in this world which is valued at[9] one hundred times sixty thousand pounds. But we are blind and in the dark. If we see a man most full of grace and virtuous, we cannot bear his perfection. If one were truly spiritual, he would hardly ever wish to see or hear any one or tarry with any one except of great necessity, but he would ever wish to remain alone."

Again he used to say of himself: "I would rather be blind than be the handsomest or richest or wisest or noblest man in the world." A certain person said to him: "Why wouldst thou rather be blind than possess these things?" He replied: "Because I fear lest they might stand in my way."

Blessed is he who will neither think nor say nor do anything blameworthy.[10]

[8] See Matt. 19:29; Mark 10:30, and Luke 18:30.
[9] F adds "more than."
[10] F, Pis., and Ed. here add the first paragraph of the following chapter without any title.

XIII

ON CONTEMPLATION

BROTHER Giles once asked a certain Brother, saying: "What do these wise men say contemplation to be?" But he said:[1] "I know not." And he (said): "Wishest thou that I tell thee what it seemeth to me?" And he (said): "I do wish." And the holy Brother Giles said: "There are seven degrees in contemplation: fire, unction, ecstasy, contemplation, taste, rest, glory.[2]

"I say 'fire,' that is, a certain light that precedeth to illumine the soul. Then the 'unction' of ointments; whence ariseth a certain wonderful odor that followeth that light, of which (it is said) in the Canticles: in 'the odor of thy ointments,' etc.[3] Then 'ecstasy'; for when the odor is felt, the soul is rapt and is withdrawn from the senses of the body. Then followeth 'contemplation'; for after it is thus withdrawn from the bodily senses, it

---

[1] Pis. for "I know not" reads: "They say many things."

[2] See "Chron. XXIV General.," p. 107, and St. Bonav. "Comment." in Luc., c. 9, n. 48 ("Opera Omnia," t. vii, p. 231), and Serm. I in Sabb. Sancto, pars, iii (l. c., t. ix, p. 269).

[3] Cant. 1: 3.

contemplateth God in a wonderful manner. Afterward followeth 'taste'; for in that contemplation it experienceth a wonderful sweetness, of which the Psalm (speaks): 'Taste and see,' etc.[4] Then 'rest,' for when the spiritual palate has been sweetened, the soul resteth in that sweetness. Lastly followeth 'glory'; because the soul glorieth in so great rest and is replenished with boundless joy; whence the Psalm: 'I shall be satisfied when thy glory shall appear.'"[5]

He also said: "No one can rise to the contemplation of the glory of the Divine Majesty except through fervor of spirit and frequent prayer. Man is quickened through fervor of spirit, and ascendeth to contemplation when the heart together with the other members is fully disposed to this in such a manner that it can wish for or think of nothing else, except of what it hath and feeleth."

The contemplative life is to leave all earthly things for the love of God, to seek only things heavenly, to pray untiringly, to read often with attention, to praise God continually by hymns and canticles.

To contemplate is to be separated from all and to be united to God alone.[6]

[4] Ps. 33 : 9.
[5] Ps. 16 : 15.
[6] This and the preceding paragraph are found in D; they are wanting in other codices; Ed. (n. 65) has the second paragraph.

He also said: "He is a good contemplator who, were he to have his hands and his feet cut off, and his eyes taken out, and his nose and ears and tongue cut off, he would care for or desire no other members and no other thing that can be thought of in the whole world except that which he hath and feeleth for the greatness of the most suave, ineffable, and inestimable odor, joy, and sweetness. Just as Mary sitting at the feet of the Lord [7] received so much of the sweetness of the word of God that she had no member that could or wished to do else than what it was doing. And this is the reason why she did not reply by any word or sign to her sister who complained that she did not aid her, for whom Christ became spokesman, answering for Mary who was unable to reply." [8]

[7] Luke 10 : 39.
[8] Several Sayings in this and the following chapter are found in other codices after chapter xxi. See Introduction, p. liv, note 107.

XIV

ON THE ACTIVE LIFE[1]

SINCE no one can enter upon the contemplative life unless he hath first been faithfully and devoutly practised in the active, it behoveth that the active life be pursued with toil and all solicitude.

He would be truly active[2] who, were it possible, would feed all the poor people of the world, would clothe all, would give them all things necessary in abundance, and would build all the churches and hospitals and bridges of this world: and if then he were considered a bad man by all people, and were he to know this well and not wish to be held otherwise than evil, and were he not on account of this to leave off from any good works, but were to practise himself in every good work with so much the more fervor, just as he who wisheth not, nor desireth, nor expecteth thence any merit in this world, considering how Martha, busy about much serving,[3] asking to be helped by her sister, was chided

---

[1] This title is found in Vat. and C.

[2] The Latin "bonus activus" I have not wit enough to translate literally.

[3] See Luke 10:41.

by the Lord, and nevertheless did not desist from her good work; thus, too, one truly active should not cease from his good work on account of any rebuke or disdain, for thence he hopeth not for an earthly but for an eternal reward.

He also said: If thou wilt find grace in prayer, pray, and if thou shalt find it not, pray; for in oblation the Lord hath accepted even the hair of goats.[4]

A king is often more pleased with the foot of one working little for him than with the whole body[5] of another working much more for him, for the Lord beholdeth the heart.[6]

When the Lord committed preaching to St. Peter, He said that He had retained the greater part[7] for Himself, saying:[8] "and thou being once converted, confirm thy brethren."[9]

---

[4] See Exod. 25:4.

[5] This is the reading of Ed., where the three last paragraphs of this chapter are found in No. 45.

[6] See I Kings 16:7.

[7] E, F, and Ed. read: "the lesser part always."

[8] See Luke 22:32.

[9] See "Chron. XXIV General.," p. 107.

XV

ON THE CONTINUAL EXERCISE OF SPIRITUAL CAUTION

IF thou wishest to see well, pluck out thy eyes and be blind; if thou wishest to hear well, be deaf; if thou wishest to walk well, cut off thy feet; if thou wishest to work well, cut off thy hands; if thou wishest to love well, hate thyself; if thou wishest to live well, die to thyself; if thou wishest to make good profit, know how to lose; if thou wishest to be rich, be poor; if thou wishest to be among delights, afflict thyself; if thou wishest to be secure, be always in fear; if thou wishest to be exalted, humble thyself; if thou wishest to be honored, despise thyself and honor those who despise thee; if thou wishest to have good, bear with evil; if thou wishest to be at rest, labor; if thou wishest to be blessed, desire to be cursed. O! what great wisdom it is to know how to do this. But since these are great things, they are not given to all.

If a man were to live a thousand years, and were to have nothing to do beyond his own lips, he would have sufficient to do within his heart; nor would he be able to come to a perfect end; so much would he have to do within his heart alone.

He who doth not make of himself two persons, a judge and a master, cannot be saved.[1]

No one should wish to see or hear anything or to speak of anything save only for his own utility, nor to proceed further in any way.

He who doth not wish to know, shall not be known; but woe to us, for those who have the gifts of the Lord do not understand (them), and those who have (them) not[2] do not seek them.

Man fashioneth God as he desireth; but He is always such as He is.[3]

---

[1] In codices Vat., C, and D, these "Sayings" are found in chapter xvii.
[2] Ed. reads: "are not known."
[3] Cf. Mal. 3:6; Heb. 1:12.

XVI

ON USEFUL AND USELESS KNOWLEDGE AND ON PREACHERS OF THE WORD OF GOD

HE who wisheth for sufficient knowledge should bow his head sufficiently and work sufficiently, and drag his belly on the ground, and the Lord will teach him sufficiently.

The greatest wisdom is to do good works, to guard oneself well, and to consider the judgments of God.

He once said to a certain person desiring to go to the schools in order to learn: "Why dost thou wish to go to the schools? The height of all knowledge is to fear and love God: these two are enough for thee. Man hath as much knowledge as he worketh good and no more. Confide not therefore in thine own wisdom, but desire to work with all care, and in these thy works place thy entire confidence; whence the Apostle: 'Let us not love in word, nor in tongue, but in deed and in truth.'"[1]

[1] I John 3 : 13.

Have not too great care to be useful to others, but be greatly concerned that thou be useful to thyself.

We sometimes desire to know much for the sake of others and little for ourselves.

The word of God belongeth not to him who heareth or speaketh it, but to him who doth it.

Many not knowing how to swim have gone into the water to aid those that were drowning, and they themselves have been lost with those that were perishing: first there was one evil and then there were two.

If thou attendest well to the salvation of thy own soul, thou wilt take good care of the salvation of all thy friends. If thou dost well thine own duty, thou wilt do rightly the duty of all thy well-wishers.

A preacher of the word of God is placed by God to be the light, example, and standard-bearer of the people of God.

Blessed is he who so directeth others on the right way that he himself doth not cease to go on the same road, and who so inviteth others to run that he himself doth not leave off running, and who so helpeth others to become rich that he himself becometh not poor thereby.

I believe that a good preacher speaketh more to himself than to others.

It seemeth to me that one who wisheth to draw the souls of sinners ought to fear much, lest he himself be drawn by them to evil. To whom a certain Brother said: "How now?" And he (said): "Turn away thine eyes that they may not behold vanity.² Those who speak do not comprehend, and those who listen do not understand."

A certain person said to him: "Which is better, to preach well, or to act well?" He answered: "Who deserveth more, one going to the house of St. James, or one showing others the way to go to St. James's?"³

I see many things that are not mine; I hear many things that I do not understand; and I say many things that I do not do: hence it seemeth to me that a man is not saved alone by sight, speech, and hearing.⁴

---

² Ps. 118:37.
³ On Giles's own pilgrimage to the shrine of St. James's see above, Introduction, p. xx.
⁴ Vat. adds "but through his own works."

XVII

ON WORDS THAT ARE GOOD AND NOT GOOD

HE who speaketh good words is as the mouth of the Lord,[1] and he who speaketh bad words is as the mouth of the devil.

When the servants of God are gathered together in any place to converse they ought to discuss the beauty of virtues so that virtues may be pleasing to them, because if they be pleasing to them they shall exercise themselves in them; and if they exercise themselves in virtues, virtues shall always be loved by them the more.

The more a man is full of vices so much the more necessary it is for him to speak of virtues. For even as one falleth into vices very easily from frequent bad discourse about vices, so one is drawn and disposed to virtues by frequent holy converse about virtues. But what shall we say? For of good we are not able to speak good, and of evil we are not able to speak evil. What, therefore, shall we say? Of good we are not able to say how

[1] See Jeremias 15:19.

good it is, nor also of the evil of guilt and punishment how evil it is, since both are incomprehensible to us.

I do not consider it to be a lesser virtue to know how to keep silence well than to know how to speak well, and it seemeth to me that a man should have a neck like that of a crane so that his speech might pass through many joints before it would proceed from his mouth.

XVIII

ON PERSEVERANCE IN GOOD

WHAT doth it profit a man to fast, to pray, to give alms, to afflict himself, to receive besides great favors from heaven, and not to reach the haven of salvation?

Behold now there appeareth on a sea a new ship, beautiful and large and full of great treasure; yet meeting with some disaster it reacheth not the haven of safety but perisheth miserably. What did all its excellence and beauty profit it? And again there is now on the sea an old ship, small, mean-looking, ill-constructed, and not filled with great treasure, and, escaping the dangers of the sea with much difficulty, it cometh safely to port; this alone is worthy of praise. It happeneth in like manner with the men of this world:[1] rightly therefore must we all fear.

---

[1] F adds: He used to say: "though a man toileth with great labor to dig up a treasure, he should guard it with greater labor and care after he hath found it. Wherefore good care is greater labor than the toil of finding."

He also used to say: "By that through which man ascendeth he descendeth, if he doth not guard himself

Though a tree be sprung up, it is not large all at once; and if large, it is not in bloom; and if in bloom, it doth not straightway produce fruit; and if it produceth fruit, the fruit is not large directly; and if large, yet not ripe; and if ripe, yet it doth not all reach the mouth to be eaten, but a great deal falleth down and rotteth, or is devoured by swine or other animals.

A certain person said to him: "May the Lord make thee end well!" Brother Giles answered: "What would it profit me had I been in quest of the kingdom of heaven for a hundred years unless I should end well. To love God and to keep oneself ever from sin I consider the two great goods of man: were one to have these two favors he would have all good."

from his foe; and by that through which he ascendeth he on the other hand ascendeth the more."

He also used to say: "If thou guardest thine eye, thou shalt have the grace of the eye, and so of the rest."

XIX

ON RELIGION[1] AND THE SAFETY THEREOF

SPEAKING of himself Brother Giles was wont to say: "I would rather have little of the grace of God in religion than much in the world, for the dangers in the world are greater and the helps fewer than in religion; but a sinful man feareth his own good rather than his own evil; since he is more afraid to do penance and to enter religion than to lie in sin and remain in the world."

A certain person of the world sought counsel from Brother Giles as to whether or not it was expedient for him to enter religion. To whom the holy Brother Giles answered: "If a very poor man were to know that a precious treasure was hidden in some public field, would he, think you, ask counsel from any one whether he should go in haste for the treasure? How much the more should men go in haste to dig up the heavenly treasure!"

---

[1] The term "religion" as here used is synonymous with the religious state or a religious order.

Of Brother Giles

When the man heard this, having sold everything, he entered religion.

Brother Giles was also wont to say: "Many enter religion and do not those things which become religion; and such are like the farmer who would put on the arms of Roland[2] and would not know how to fight with them; for all men do not know how to ride the horse Bayard,[3] nor when sitting on him do they know how to avoid mishaps. I do not consider it a great thing to enter the court of a king, nor do I think it a great thing to receive gifts from a king, but I do esteem it a great thing to know how to behave in the royal court as it becometh. The court of the Great King is religion, to enter which and to receive of the gifts of God in it is not a great thing, but (it is a great thing) to know how to live

---

[2] Roland, called by Italians Orlando, was a paladin of the court of Charlemagne and one of the most famous heroes of chivalry in medieval romance. The "Song of Roland" a metrical narrative of his chief exploits, and which formed part of the "chansons de geste," was a favorite with the minstrels of the Middle Ages. It was probably after his entrance into the Order, as Le Monnier remarks, that Giles read the "Song of Roland," for St. Francis opened to his disciples the sources from which he himself had drawn. See "Spec. Perf." (ed. Sabatier), c. iv, pp. 10-11.

[3] Roland's horse, Bayard — so named from its color — would not suffer any save the four sons of Haymon to ride it. See Du Cange: "Glossar." v. Bayard; see also Bartsch: "Das Rolandslied." Leipzig, 1874, p. 70, note on v, 1649.

in it and devoutly and anxiously persevere unto the end, as it becometh. For I would rather live in the world and devoutly and anxiously yearn to enter religion, than be in religion and be wearied of it."

The glorious Virgin Mary, Mother of God, was born of a sinful race, nor was she in any religion, and yet she is what she is.

A religious should believe that he knoweth not how to live and that he cannot live save in religion.[4]

He once likewise said to a certain companion of his: "From the beginning of the world up to the present time a better or surer religion hath not appeared than the religion of the Friars Minor."[5]

He also said: "It seemeth to me that the religion of the Friars Minor was truly sent into this world for the great benefit of man; but woe to us unless we are such men as we should be. The religion of the Friars Minor seemeth to me to be the richest and poorest in the world, but this seemeth to me to be our greatest vice that we desire to soar too high. He is rich who imitateth the rich man; he

---

[4] Vat., C, D add: "It is a great virtue to permit oneself to be despised by men; because the more one alloweth himself to be despised, the more is he lord of this world."

[5] F in place of "Minor" reads "nec in tantum." Then it adds: "He who goeth to religion is like an unarmed man and fleeth to a strong and fortified citadel."

is wise who imitateth the wise man; he is good who imitateth the good man; he is handsome who imitateth the handsome man; he is noble who imitateth Him who is noble, namely, our Lord Jesus Christ."

XX

ON OBEDIENCE AND ITS UTILITY[1]

THE more a religious is held beneath the yoke of obedience for the love of God, so much the greater fruit will he reap; and the more a religious is obedient and subject to his superior for the honor of God, so much the more is he poor and free from his sin in comparison with all the other men of this world.[2]

A truly obedient religious is like a soldier well-armed seated upon a good horse who

---

[1] Two incidents related in "Chron. XXIV. General." have a special interest by the light of this chapter. It is recorded that, while walking one day near Agello with a companion, Blessed Giles received a summons from the Minister General to go to Assisi. At once he turned in that direction, nor could his companion, who urged him to first return to the convent where he had been staying, obtain from him any other answer than this: " Brother, I am commanded to go to Assisi, not to the convent." And when a Friar complained to Blessed Giles on another occasion that he was sent from prayer to beg alms and was thus obliged to leave the greater good for the lesser, the holy man replied: " Brother, believe me, thou knowest not yet what prayer is, for the most true and perfect thing is to do the will of thy Superior." See " Chron. XXIV General.," p. 80.

[2] Vat., Is., and C add: " The most wicked devils of hell are dissemblers of great subjection."

passeth safely among the enemies and no one can harm him, but the religious who obeyeth murmuringly is like an unarmed soldier seated upon a poor horse who, passing among the enemy, falleth and is at once taken by the foe, chained, wounded, imprisoned, and then put to death.

A religious who desireth to live according to his own will desireth to go into hell fire.

So long as the ox holdeth its head beneath the yoke it filleth the granaries with grain, but the ox not holding its head beneath the yoke but running about wandering seemeth to itself to be a great lord, but the granaries are not filled with grain.

The great and the wise humbly put their heads beneath the yoke of obedience, and the foolish withdraw their heads from beneath the yoke and will not obey.

A mother sometimes nourisheth and maketh much of her son who after he hath grown up doth not obey his mother on account of his pride, but mocketh and spurneth her.[3]

I esteem it greater to obey a superior for the love of God than to obey the Creator Himself giving some command in person.[4]

---

[3] D adds: "The mother is religion; the son is the religious who, nourished and made much of by her, afterward despiseth and mocketh her and doth not wish to be obedient."

[4] Ed. omits the rest of this chapter.

However, it seemeth to me that if one were in such great grace that he might speak with the angels, if he were called by a man to whom he had promised obedience, he ought to leave off his colloquy with the angels and obey the man, because while he is subject in this world he is bound to obey the man to whom he is subject, on account of the Creator.[5] And the reason is that the Lord, as we read in the first book of Kings,[6] did not manifest His will to Samuel before he had permission from Heli.

He who placeth his head beneath the yoke of obedience, and afterward that he may follow the path of perfection withdraweth his head from beneath the yoke of obedience — this is a sign of great hidden pride.

Good habits are the way to all good, and bad habits are the way to all evil.

[5] In this connexion see what is related of Brother Andrew, Giles's companion, in "Chron. XXIV. General.," p. 100.

[6] See I Kings, 3.

XXI

ON THE RECOLLECTION OF DEATH

IF one had lived from the beginning of the world until now and had continuously suffered evil during his whole life and presently he should attain to all good, what harm would all the evil he had suffered do him? And if one should always have had every good from the beginning of the world until now and presently should come to all evil, what would all the good he has had profit him?

A certain secular said to him: "I wish to live long in this world and to have all things in plenty." To whom he replied: "If thou shouldst live for a thousand years and shouldst be the lord of the whole world, what reward wouldst thou receive at thy death from the flesh which thou hast served? But in a little while he who behaveth rightly and guardeth himself well shall receive an unfailing reward in the future."[1]

---

[1] Codex G and the St. Isidore MS. 1/82 end here.

XXII

ON SHUNNING THE WORLD[1]

GOOD company is to man like an antidote and bad company like poison.

Trees which stand by the way and at the crossroads are sometimes struck with a sword by the wayfarers, and the fruit is not suffered to ripen: even so is it hurtful to abide in public.

---

[1] The titles of this and the following chapters are from cod. Vat.; in other MSS. they are without titles. Ed. contains these two chapters under n. 54. In Is., F, Pis., and Ed. those Sayings which are given above in chapters xiii and xiv follow the chapter on "The Recollection of Death." See Introduction, p. lvi, note 107.

XXIII

ON PERSEVERANCE IN PRAYER

SOMEONE said to Brother Giles: "What can I do that I may feel some of the sweetness of God?" He replied: "Hath God ever inspired thee with a good will?" Who said: "Quite often." Brother Giles spoke to him in these words, crying out with a loud voice: "Why didst thou not keep that good will and it would have led thee to a greater good?"

Another said: "What shall I do for I am dry and indevout?" He answered him ironically: "Do not pray to God nor offer thy gift at the altar. When the force of overflowing water breaketh through the mill pond and altogether destroyeth the mill-race, the miller striveth by degrees to mend those things which have been broken down; and likewise when the stones of the mill do not make good flour, he doth not thereupon smash them with a large hammer, but with a small one he gently and gradually striketh them until they are mended." [1]

[1] See above, p. 41.

Religious have been called by God for the most part to give themselves to prayer, humility, and fraternal[2] charity; but woe to them who have lost the desire of their good and who wish to go too high.[3]

[2] Vat. reads "supernal."
[3] Many MSS. with Pis. (c. 22) and Ed. (n. 66) before the following chapter put the chapter " De Virtutibus," which is wanting in codd. of class A ; it is omitted here because the "Sayings" it contains are found in other chapters (in chap. i, p. 81; chap. i, p. 85; chap. xvii, and chap. x). Cod. D contains the following which are not found elsewhere: "A man who desireth to seek God aright, should do as the small boy doth when his mother leaveth him — who is consoled by nothing unless he have his mother again and who seeketh her with such eagerness that he seemeth to be losing his life. And if all the gold in the world were given him and if he were to become an emperor and all men were to desire to serve and honor him as much as they could, he would consider all these things as nothing unless he were to have his mother again. Thus he should do who desireth to seek Jesus Christ.

"O! unhappy man, look about thee; think, consider thy miseries, for thou art blind, poor, and naked. And if thou esteemedst thyself blind, thou wouldst ask the King of kings to enlighten thee; if poor, thou wouldst at once beg food; if naked, thou wouldst seek clothing; go therefore to the fountain of graces and virtues and ask something from Him, for he who asketh, receiveth, and he who seeketh, findeth, and to him who knocketh, it shall be opened. Ask by prayer, seek by the desire of love, knock by perseverance." "O! unhappy man," etc., is also found in F.

XXIV

ON THE GRACES AND VIRTUES WHICH ARE ACQUIRED IN PRAYER

THE graces and virtues which are merited and found in prayer are many. The first is, that man is enlightened in mind; the second, that he is strengthened in faith; the third, that he knoweth his own miseries; the fourth, that he arriveth at holy fear and is humiliated and becometh despicable in his own eyes; the fifth, that he attaineth to contrition of heart; the sixth, that he is purified in conscience;[1] the seventh, that he is confirmed in patience; the eighth, that he placeth himself under obedience; the ninth, that he cometh to true discretion;[2] the tenth, that he attaineth knowledge; the eleventh, that he cometh to understanding; the twelfth, that he acquireth fortitude; the thirteenth, that he attaineth wisdom; the fourteenth, that he arriveth at the knowledge of God who manifesteth Himself to those that

---

[1] Here cod. D, F, Pis. and Ed. add: "the sixth, because tears of sorrow flow; seventh, because he arriveth at amendment of heart; eighth, because he is purified in conscience," etc.

[2] Pis. and Ed. for discretion read "obedience."

adore Him in spirit and in truth.³ Then man is inflamed with love, runneth in the odor, and attaineth to the suavity, of sweetness, is led to peace of mind, and finally cometh to glory. But after he shall have placed his mouth to the words of the Most High where the soul is filled, who shall be able to separate him from prayer which hath led him to such contemplation? Hence, Gregory (saith): heavenly sweetness having been tasted, "all things that are on earth become sordid." ⁴

But in order that one may arrive at the foregoing, six other things are necessary: first, namely consideration of one's own past evils for which it behoveth one to be sorry; secondly, caution concerning present evils; thirdly, fear of future evils; fourthly, consideration of the mercies of God who awaiteth man, not avenging Himself for his sins, since for each mortal sin man is worthy according to Divine Justice of eternal punishment; fifthly, consideration of the benefits of God which cannot be explained, namely, the benefits of the flesh which He assumed for us, of the passion which He suffered for us, of the teaching which He left us; sixthly, of the glory which He hath promised us.⁵

---

³ John 4:24.
⁴ See "II Homil. in Evang.," hom. 37, n. 1 (P. L. 76, 1626).
⁵ Pis. and Ed. continue as follows: "He also said: 'Those things which a secular hateth, the religious

should love, namely, poverty, shame, nakedness, hunger, thirst, lowliness and the like.'

"The holy Brother Giles said of the religion: 'The ship is wrecked; it hath broken up; let him flee who may flee and escape if he be able.'" (See "Chron. XXIV General.," p. 86.) Then follow in Pis. and Ed. what is contained below, p. 91.

XXV

ON THE NEGLIGENCE OF PRELATES[1] IN THE CANONIZATION OF CERTAIN FRIARS[2]

IT seemed to Brother Giles that the higher prelates of the Order of Friars Minor acted wrongly in that they did not bring about with all their might before the Lord Pope — not indeed for the sake of their own glory, but considering only the honor of the Lord and the edification of their neighbors — to obtain the canonization of the Friars Minor martyrs who were killed at Morocco for their glorious confession of the faith.[3] And if the Lord Pope should have wished to canonize them, it were indeed well; but if not, the Brothers seeking this would be excused before God. And he added: "If we had not the example

---

[1] By prelates are understood the major superiors of the Order, such as ministers or guardians.
[2] This title is taken from C and H. This and the following chapter (xxv and xxvi) are wanting in F and Pis.; in Ed. they are found under Nos. 57 and 58.
[3] The *Passio* of these protomartyrs of the Order who suffered at Morocco in 1220 may be read in "Anal. Francis.," t. iii, p. 579 ff. Their feast is celebrated on 16 January.

of the fathers who have gone before us, perhaps we should not be in the state of penance in which we are; but God rendereth to each one gold for gold, scarlet for scarlet, a lock of hair for a lock of hair, nor doth any one do one thing for God but that God doth another for him."

XXVI

HOW BLESSED BROTHER GILES SETTLED SUNDRY NOTEWORTHY QUESTIONS[1]

AT one time the holy Brother Giles was bewailing the great besiegement of a certain city[2] which had been revealed to him, grieving both for the cruelty of the conquerors and for the danger of the oppressed. And after he said that we ought to grieve much over these things he added, speaking in these words: "God wished, however, that the men of that city should be punished and humiliated, because they often treated their neighbors, than whom they were stronger, cruelly enough."

A certain religious then said to him: "If God willed that, we ought not to pity them as thou sayest, but rather to rejoice in their punishment, since every man should conform his will to the Divine Will." To whom the holy Brother Giles replied: "Let us suppose

---

[1] This title is taken from codex H.
[2] It is not easy to determine what city is here alluded to. The Bollandists think it may refer to Rome, which for two months, in 1243, was besieged by the Emperor Frederic.

that a king issued an edict that whosoever should commit a certain crime be beheaded or hanged, and supposing that the king's son committing the self same crime is led forth by the king's mandate to the death aforesaid — believest thou that it would please the king for men to rejoice and say: 'Let us be glad, for the lord king leadeth his son to death'? Such rejoicing would not please the king but would rather displease him; even so," he said, "it is in this case."

On another occasion some one said to Brother Giles: "If one praiseth me for the good I know I do not possess, for that do I glory vainly in my heart." Brother Giles answered: "If some one were most poor, wounded all over, and pale, miserable, and clothed in filthy garments and altogether barefoot, and men should come to him saying: 'Hail, my lord, for thou art wondrous rich, handsome, and fair, and wearest most fine apparel,' would not he be a fool if such praise pleased him, and if he deemed himself to be what they said of him when he knew for certain that the case was quite otherwise?"

APPENDICES

APPENDIX I

I

ON THE FEAR OF GOD[1]

A MAN should do a hundred things for fear more willingly than one for love, because true fear is born of true love; which true and most high fear no one can have except through the most high and true love of God; because a true and holy fear driveth out every other fear and maketh itself obeyed by the ones fearing, and causeth them ever to bow their heads to the ground under the yoke of obedience; because holy fear then clearly showeth what great love it hath toward God by humbling and conquering itself to obey not only the Creator, but also any creature. To possess this fear and love is a very great gift of God: hence it is not given to all.[2]

The greater the gifts the Lord conferreth upon His servant, so much the more ungrateful is he if he doth not return Him thanks. Hence it is perilous to ask virtues of God, because if thou workest not according to the

---

[1] The Sayings in this chapter are from MSS. of the collection A in which they follow chapter xxiv.

[2] See above, p. 15.

grace given thee, thou becomest a greater enemy of God by reason of ingratitude.[3]

Brother Giles used to say [4] that sins are like burs which stick fast to the clothes and can with difficulty be removed.

If thou leavest me in peace, it is well with thee; if thou annoyest me, it is ill with thee.

Brother Giles once said to a certain Brother: "Which among all the trees thou beholdest seemeth to thee the most beautiful?" The Brother replied: "I have seen a very beautiful fir tree and a beech tree." Who said: "What fruit doth it produce? But the vine produceth liquid fruit, which is trodden and cellared and ever becometh better, so that it changeth man and leadeth him beyond himself. What, then, is there to wonder at if the Creator draweth a man beyond himself?"

He likewise said: "A good soul [5] is, as it were, a small cask of wine in fermentation; but of what hindrance are the fastenings of the cask itself to the working of the wine?"

Again he said to a certain Brother: "Didst thou ever see a great tree?" Who said: "I have seen one." And he said: "When that great tree began to spring forth from the earth, I would have been able to uproot it

---

[3] This paragraph is found in MSS. of the class B in the chapter "De Virtutibus" (see above, p. 70, note 3).

[4] The following Sayings are also found in C.

[5] The Latin text here seems to be corrupted. Vat. for "soul" reads "grape"; but C with greater probability reads "bona anima," as above.

Appendix I

with two fingers. But now what? A single creature could have then done it more harm than the whole world could do it now."

Someone said to him: "Against what vice ought man to fight most?" He answered: "Close up the cask in that place whence the wine escapeth: even so fight against that vice which besetteth thee the most."

A certain person said to him: "Why did John the Baptist lead so hard a life when he was young?" He replied: "Why are meats salted? Not because they are rotten, but that the bad humors may be dried up, lest they putrify and become wormy, and that they may be more tasty." [6]

Blessed is he who striveth to conquer himself.

Our flesh is like Baldach [7] of the Saracens: against it we need to wage war untiringly.

If man did not prepare a place for God within himself, he would not find a place among the creatures of God. [8]

A certain person said to him: "Brother Giles, I was seeking thee, desiring to speak to thee." To whom Brother Giles answered: "If thou shouldst see the sun, thou wouldst care little about the dawn. The sun is Christ, who must be sought." And he said: "For if all the beauties which God hath made and the

---

[6] See "Chron. XXIV General.," p. 109.

[7] An allusion to the powerful kingdom of that name. See Golubovich, 1. c., p. 263: Littré, "Dict. Suppl. Orient."; v. Baldaquin.

[8] See above, p. 26.

sweet-smelling things were gathered together in one place, who could bear them? What, therefore, must we think of the Creator of all things?"

If some one speaketh well to thee and thou shalt have answered well, it is well for him and for thee; and if some one speaketh ill to thee and thou shalt have answered ill, it is ill for him and for thee; and if some one should speak ill to thee and thou shalt have answered well, it will be well for thee and ill for him.

He once said to a certain Brother thus: "The holy David uttered three words in the Psalms which no one can fully understand unless he have the spirit of him who spoke them. The first is this: 'O, how great is the multitude of Thy sweetness,' etc.[9] The second is this: 'O, taste and see that the Lord is sweet.'[10] The third is this: 'Much peace have they that love Thy law, and to them there is no stumbling-block.'"[11]

The greatest grace that man can have under heaven is to know how to live well with those among whom he dwelleth.

Two noblewomen asked Brother Giles to speak a few good words to them. Who said: "On what matter do we desire to speak? If we speak of the temporal things of this world, they are empty; if we speak of the works of the flesh, they are foul and filthy; if, however, we desire to speak of God, who knoweth how to speak of Him as it becometh, and who may understand him who speaketh thus?" And he

[9] Ps. 30 : 20.   [10] Ps. 33 : 9.   [11] Ps. 118 : 165.

was straightway rapt in ecstasy; and one of the noblewomen said: "I grieve that he hath spoken so little to us;" the other replied: "He said in a few words whatever was needful."

On another occasion [12] he said: "Graces and virtues are at hand for all creatures, calling all and saying: 'Come and receive us, for we will teach you the way of truth'; and miserable man doth not wish to go. Whose fault is it, then, if miserable man always liveth in wretchedness and poverty, since he is called to the Lord and doth not wish to labor by going to Him; and hence he is worthy of everlasting punishments." [13]

---

[12] In MSS. of Class B the following paragraph is found in chap. "De Virtutibus" (see above, p. 70, note 3).

[13] Cod. Vat. ends here as follows: "Here end a few words of the holy Brother Giles which his companions heard from his lips"; so also cod. 12, Liegnitz. See "Opuscules de critique hist.," t. i, p. 54.

II

OF THOSE WHO ARE IN FAVOR AND DISFAVOR WITH GOD[1]

AMONG all religions and religious some please God, and some displease Him. But those who please Him are of two orders: one is called the order of those who love; the other of those who please.

Now in the order of lovers are all the great servants of God who wholly love themselves in the desire of pleasing God and who love one another in the desire of pleasing one another for God's sake. These lovers have four eyes: one eye ever regardeth what is most pleasing to the will and good pleasure of the Lord God; the other always regardeth the neighbor to be ever at peace with him and show him good example. Of the other two, one looketh forward, the other backward. The one that is before, looketh at what is likely to happen in every work that it doth; that which is behind, considereth if the work which it doth pleaseth the Lord God. And thus the eye that is before looketh backward and that

---

[1] This chapter which is found in MSS. of class B is wanting a title in the Latin. In Ed. it is contained under numbers 59-62.

which is behind looketh before, and these two eyes are the judges of works.

The other order is called that of those who please, and all those are called pleasers who watch themselves lest they say or do any harm to another; and if others do them wrong, they become the servants of those who afflict them with entire good will of heart, and they go, that is, according to justice, and do not go beyond the limits of justice, that they may reckon with some one. These two orders are in the good favor of the Lord God.

But those religious who live in discord and contention, on account of earthly things, and not because of the good of the soul, but who for the sake of security esteem themselves good — all are in disfavor with the Lord God; but they can return from disfavor into His good grace by penance and confession and caution. But let them beware, because they may persevere so long in evildoing that the gate of mercy may be closed to them and they be cast beyond salvation.

And prelates, masters of divinity, preachers, and priests are constituted by God for this reason, that they should know how to draw souls to salvation, and that they should desire and seek this more eagerly than they drink water or wine when they thirst exceedingly, and that they should undergo suffering for souls. Such masters, preachers, and priests are all in the favor of the Lord God. But all such masters, preachers, and priests as thirst more to be praised and honored than they thirst to draw souls to salvation, all stand in disfavor with God; but they may return from this disfavor to the favor of God if they confess and thenceforth watch themselves. But they may remain so long in this state that the gate of mercy may be closed upon them and they be cast out beyond salvation.

The Lord causeth all peoples to be born for His own honor and for this reason that they should all love Him above all things, and their neighbor as themselves for His sake.

In so far doth one nation love another as they cherish and exhort each other to be saved.

Every nation which doth not love and fear God is in mortal sin, and is given into the hand of hate and thrown beyond salvation.

Every nation which groweth great in its own estimation and reputeth itself to be mighty and good in this that it is of God, and doth not recognize that what it hath is from God, the same, willing or unwilling, He shall belittle and humiliate.

Every nation that will not do penance and satisfy for sins, is given into the hand of punishment and is thrown beyond salvation into damnation.

Every nation that doth not fear God and tremble before Him, is given into the hand of great trembling and thrown beyond salvation into damnation.

These nations which love earthly things more than the Lord who made them, shall be punished in suffering and stripes.

These nations which do not love their own

good, that is the salvation of their soul, shall possess their evil, that is the damnation of their soul.

Every nation that will not hear of, nor observe, its relation to God, is ordained to punishment.

Every nation that mocketh the word of God is ordained to the punishment of anger.

As when the sun riseth, the stars lose their light in presence of the sun, so do the moon and sun lose their light in presence of one glorified soul.

It is one sign that man is in the grace of God, if he is exalted in nothing, but always humiliated.

But I excuse myself before God and you, for it is not I who say the foregoing, because of myself I would be hung up on forks and hurled beyond salvation into damnation.

There are eight precious stones which the Lord hath given to the holy hermits, to Blessed Francis, to Blessed Dominic, as also to holy monks, and to all His saints. The first is, to be sorry for one's sins and to confess them uprightly and to do penance for them, and to beware of future sins and to be obedient. The second is, that the saints themselves were uprooted from all hope of the world or of men, so that their hearts finding no root of temporality or fleshliness where they were placed, necessarily reverted to God above who had made their hearts. The third is, that they recognized that all the good they had was from God, and every evil from their sins. The fourth, that if any said or did injury to them they served them out of an entire good will of heart. The fifth, that they loved blame and not honors, and loved unity of penance in every people, and that they were merciful and pious. The sixth, that they esteemed themselves viler than all others and all others better than they. Seventh, that they served themselves and did not expect to be served; and whoever esteemed them as vile, they with the latter esteemed themselves as vile. Eighth, that they recognized that benefits were from God, and they returned them to Him, saying, "Lord, what are we? for if Thou withdrawest from us Thy goods which Thou hast given us, we shall be worse than all who are in the Provinces." For whoever appropriateth to himself the goods which are God's, God despoileth him of them, and who appropriateth nothing to himself, but attributeth all to God, to him God appropriateth his goods which he doth.[2]

[2] E adds: "Here end the Golden Words of Brother Giles."

III

ADMONITIONS ON PREACHING AND WORKING [1]

HE also used often to say with fervor of spirit: "Paris, Paris, thou destroyest the Order of St. Francis."

In like manner he once instructed a certain (friar) preaching in the piazza of Perugia to say, "Bo bo, molto dico e poco fo." "I say much and do little." [2]

When he heard the master of a vineyard near which he dwelt saying to the laborers in the vineyard the word "Faite," going forth from his cell he called out in fervor of spirit: "Hear ye, Brothers, the word that ought to be: Work! work! and talk not!" [3]

He also used to say: [4] "The more any one would love the good of another above that

---

[1] From Codex C, where, however, they are wanting a title.

[2] Pis. and Ed. omit "often," "once," and "in the piazza of Perugia," and give the Latin words as well as the Italian.

[3] Pis. and Ed. give the Latin words as well as the Italian here also. The three foregoing Sayings, Pis. puts in the last chapter; Ed. in n. 68 (see "Chron. XXIV General.," p. 86).

[4] The two following paragraphs are also found in the Vita B. Aegidii (Ed. Lemmens. See "Doc. Ant. Franc.," t. i, p. 37).

which the Lord worketh in himself, so much the more will that good be made his, so long as he knoweth to trade with it and gain by it, and guard it, for good is not of man but of God."

He likewise said: "Since I am not spiritual as I should be, and do not love greatly and rejoice in the good of another and am not saddened at and have no compassion in the suffering and evil of another, nay even from the good and evil of another whence I should profit I do not profit, therefore do I offend charity, is my good lessened, and do I fall into sin."

IV

ON GOOD WORKS AND CORRESPONDENCE WITH GRACE [1]

THOU oughtest to ask God that He do thee not much good in this world, and that He send thee to hard battles, and that He aid thee not, because of the greater reward.

He also used to say: "In this may it be known whether any one perfectly loveth God, if in every care he separateth himself the more from his vices, and daily performeth good works the more."

And again he said: "In religions it is to-day as it was in the primitive Church, when men were converted to the faith who were fervent in undergoing martyrdom, but after [the era of] martyrdom ceased they became cold. So it is to-day in religions: we in the beginning of our vocation and conversion were fervent in doing fruitful and bitter penance, but after a time we became cold and lukewarm."

This is one of the greatest benefits of God, namely, to guard the grace given to one by God and to know how to profit and trade in good works and to flee from sins.

---

[1] From Cod. Is. Pis. has nearly all this chapter in his last chapter, Ed. in Nos. 69 and 70.

He also used to say: "It is a greater virtue to follow up grace than to bear sufferings patiently, for many bear sufferings patiently but do not follow up grace."

He also said: "A Friar Minor is only to be spoken of as of one, namely, subject beneath the feet of all; because the greater the descent so much the greater the ascent. Wherefore the Blessed Francis used to say that it had been revealed to him by the Lord that they should be called Friars Minor." [2]

He also said: "He who loveth the more yearneth the more."

He likewise said: "We ought to be more afraid of goods than of evils. Man," he said, "followeth evil, but is contrary to good."

We ought so to converse with men as not to lose what the Lord worketh in us. And let us strive that we may know how to save ourselves with the few. For it often happeneth that he who knoweth how to swim, if he knoweth not wisely and cautiously how to help another who is in danger of perishing in the water, is himself in danger lest they both perish and die.[3]

He also said that man will be held to give an account of the grace which he hath not, for since the Lord createth His creature through

---

[2] The last sentence in this paragraph is omitted in Pis. and Ed. See "Doc. Ant. Francis.," t. i, p. 85; see also "The Origin of the Name Friar Minor," by Montgomery Carmichael, in "Franciscan Monthly," October, 1904.

[3] See above, p. 54. Cod. 1/89 St. Isid. ends here.

Appendix I 95

His benevolence and grace, he even from his nature should be benevolent and full of grace. Hence man loseth his perfection through his negligence and imperfection; for if he laboreth well and carefully in the grace given to him, he would find that the grace for which he hopeth would be given to him.[4]

It is better to be in the house of God, that is in religion, filled with serpents, if God be there, than to be in a beautiful house filled with delights and riches without the Divine Presence.

He used likewise to say: "I wish," he said, "to have this perfection until death: first, to be obedient in all things until death; secondly, I wish to be subject beneath the feet of others; thirdly, I wish to rebuke and chastise myself severely; fourthly, I wish to lacerate my flesh with my teeth; fifthly, if I should voluntarily wish to withdraw myself from these things, I wish to be dragged by a cord around the neck."[5]

---

[4] Pis. and Ed. for "which he hopeth" read "which he hath not."

[5] Pis. and Ed.: "I do not wish to withdraw myself from these; I wish them to drag me by force with a cord around my neck."

The codex adds: "Here end some very useful words of the holy Brother Giles which companions heard from his lips. But the holy Brother Giles lived fifty-three years less one day in the Order, for he went to Blessed Francis at St. Mary of the Porziuncula on the day of St. George, and on the Vigil of St. George he went to the Lord. And when he first went to Blessed Francis, Blessed Francis had but two friars only, namely, the holy

Brother Bernard of Quintavalle and another brother who was called Brother Peter. And thus the holy Brother Giles was the fourth Friar Minor, and all these were from Assisi. To the praise and glory and honor of our Lord Jesus Christ, who with the Father and the Holy Ghost liveth and reigneth world without end. Amen."

V

ON GRATITUDE AND CONTRITION [1]

IN like manner Brother Giles said in the presence of certain lectors: "I," he said, "would willingly possess two things in myself, namely, to learn to praise God for the favors bestowed upon me, and to be sorry for my sins: and these would be sufficient for me until the day of death."

He also said: "In order that a man divest himself of the goods which the Lord worketh in him, it behoveth first that he ever render the goods of the Lord to the Lord alone, to whom they belong; secondly, that he hold himself guilty and a sinner in everything, and that he ought not to defend himself save from heresy."

He also said that a man should not only bear injuries and insults patiently, but even with joy of soul and body, he ought to offer a gift to those who say hurtful words to him or do him evil because of the great reward which followeth thence.

[1] From Codex F, of which the text seems much corrupted. After chap. xxiv this codex puts the last four paragraphs given above in chap. ix, following which come the "Sayings" contained in the present chapter. I have taken the liberty of giving a title to this as well as to the three preceding chapters.

There was a certain religious of great abstemiousness who Brother Giles feared would go mad; wherefore he said: "The emperors, kings, and magnates do not give great gifts to fools and simpletons, but to the wise."

He also said: "The servant of God worketh the more to find and have humility, since humility knoweth not how to speak and is nothing, in that the truly humble man esteemeth himself as nothing, for the more any one esteemeth himself mean and vile, so much the more shall he find and gain the virtue of humility and be exalted by God."

In like manner the Lord said to His disciples: "Others have labored and you have entered into their labors":[2] for although the apostles labored not less than the prophets, yet the Lord to preserve the humility of His disciples said: "And when you have done all these things that I have told you, say: We are unprofitable servants."[3]

He also said: "The Lord was born under the earth, namely, in a cave, received gifts from the Magi, fled into Egypt; He teacheth us that we should be humble and lowly, bowing to every creature."

We ought to receive His grace from Him, which he willingly giveth, because for that He created us. Afterward we ought to follow it up with good works: wherefore, the Lord saith: "Trade till I come."[4] We ought to flee vices and sins.

---

[2] John 4:38.   [3] See Luke 17:10.   [4] Luke 19:13.

He also said to a certain Brother: "Thou," he said, "shouldst desire that every man speak ill of thee."

He likewise said to the same: "We can be martyrs without the sword and shedding of blood," and he said, "by holy devotion, joy, and cheerfulness a man deserveth to gain merit and the crown of martyrdom."

He also said that a man ought to love one creature more than another in so far as the Lord worketh more in one than in another, and in so far as man is more edified by one than by the other.

When too he had asked a certain man whether he believed in God, and the same had said that he did, he said: "I shall show thee how much thou believest. Suppose that thou wert passing through a great city, and at the first step thou shouldst meet some one who with angry face and in great rage would say something very injurious to thee, and, at the second step, one who would speak to thee twice as badly and with twofold wrath and fury; at the third, one who would speak to thee thrice as badly, and so on, until the city gate — I say to thee, my son, that inasmuch as thou shouldst persevere in that belief, so much faith hast thou and no more, for faith would not endure without work."

In like manner when he had asked some one whether one time were better for man than another, and the latter had said that it was, because at one time one may work better than in another, he (Giles) said: "At all times the

Lord is ready to do good to the creature, if the creature knew how to understand and receive."

He also said: "Man loseth his perfection on account of negligence."

He also said: "To blame oneself and to praise another, to speak well of another and badly of oneself — this is a great virtue."

He also said: "God created man through His kindness, grace, and love; therefore man of his nature ought to be kind and full of grace."[5]

He also said: "Man is a noble creature of God; but without grace he is nothing, because without grace he blindeth, chaineth, and even slayeth another. For example, what is the earth worth unless it bringeth forth its fruit? But the grace of God maketh just men and saints of this sort of sinners."

He also said: "If we saw a very lovable man most gracious, most virtuous, we could not bear his perfection because of frailty of the body and weakness of spirit."

He also said: "All things proceed from prayer and it is the beginning and the end of every good."[6]

He also said that a spiritual man fleeth familiarities and always desireth to be alone.

In like manner, being asked what was the greater virtue, custody of the tongue or the bridling of (this) member, he afterward said that was the greater in which a man was most attacked.

[5] See Ed., No. 70.   [6] See above, p. 40.

He also said: "The highest wisdom is to do good and to watch oneself, and to consider the judgments of God."

He also said: "He who is humble and quiet whilst he is satisfied may not thence have graces and praise."

He also said: "Through that by which man ascendeth by the same he descendeth, if he doth not guard himself from the opposite; and, on the other hand, through that by which he descendeth he ascendeth the more."

He also said: "A man is not to be called blessed if he hath a good will, unless he followeth it up, because for this the Lord giveth it him — that he follow it up."

He also said: "When any one is associated with another, though he may tattle and weary the latter, yet he should not send him away on this account, because he is much to be commended and his reward daily increaseth in that he resisteth the flesh even to the end."

He also said: "There is nothing left save that a man should gain a victory over himself, for it is a small thing to draw souls, unless he vanquisheth himself."

He also said: "Every good which thou hast not, thou oughtest to consider and esteem great and wonderful in him who hath it: after thou attainest to that, thou oughtest to consider and regard it as greater in another than in thyself."

He also said: "Have grace and follow it up by trading with it in good works. Be virtuous and fight bravely against vices."

He also said: "One man is ignorant of all the arts; but another more, another less, according to the will and good pleasure of the Giver."

He also said: "Whilst man liveth, even the perfect religious is unarmed, for there is no perfect security so long as man is among enemies. The flesh is the greatest enemy, and with the devil it is ever opposed to the soul."

He also said: "We labor in the doctrine of the Lord which has been from Adam until the Lord's coming, in which holy men and women have labored faithfully and courageously, and those things which they have not been able to do in works they fulfilled by holy desires and good will: but we labor carelessly; wherefore we must fear."

He also said: "The highest, fairest, and most splendid things which are above man must be hoped for; wherefore consider Mary and Martha."

He also said: "The Lord would gladly bestow His treasure upon men if He found receptacles ready."

He also said: "All creatures that would be saved must of necessity return to prayer in the end."[7]

He also said: "Whatever is done without love and devotion is not pleasing to God and the saints."[8]

He also said: "A man who loseth the good of all goods which all the angels and saints of heaven cannot restore to him — how can any

---

[7] See above, p. 40.   [8] See above, p. 10.

one console him? No one, save the Divine Clemency." [9]

No one can merit or claim the kingdom of heaven, but he can seek it.

Some one also said: "If I could see the merit of good works, I would willingly exercise myself in good works." Giles replied: "Look at the lovers of worldly things: how long they labor before they see and partake of the fruit of their labors! If, therefore, they toil thus for transitory things, how much more should one labor for eternal things? No one, while he liveth, can see the great things of God. It behoveth us therefore to labor carefully not for those things which are seen with fleshly eyes, but hoping in the Lord, for whatever is seen is nothing in respect of those things which cannot be seen."

A certain person questioned him, saying: "What can I do that I may know what is most useful and salutary for my soul?" And answering, he said: "If thou wishest to know much, strive to bow thy head much and to drag thy belly along the ground." "How may I do this?" He replied: "If thou art not the king, thou oughtest to believe that some one is king. What thou hast not, another hath. Besides, thou oughtest to reverence much the grace which another hath, which also, if thou shouldst have, thou oughtest to esteem greater in another than in thyself."

A man feareth and dreadeth and hateth his

---

[9] See above, p. 8, where the same idea is somewhat differently expressed.

own good more than any other thing in the world. For he feareth to do penance and to enter religion, where a multitude of graces and virtues is found which maketh the precepts of the Lord easy and sweet to observe. For I firmly believe and I know that he who experienceth the love of the Most High is not cast down by work or labor; because where love is, there is no labor. For if a tradesman should sell his wares for more than a hundred times their value, although he should, in furthering their sale, have undergone trouble, as, for example, heat, cold, waiting, worry, and toil, he would withal esteem the labor as nothing, nay, he would not consider labor as labor, but as a consolation. If, then, a man delighteth in temporal works, forgetful of labor in the desire of gain, how much [should we not labor] for eternal things?

A certain other person asked: " Can any one find grace in the world?" Who said: "He can. For my part I would prefer one grace in religion to ten in the world. I mean the grace of prayer, of fasting, of silence, and the like. For the grace found in religion is easily kept when the religious is separated from the noise and the crowd of worldly care,—the enemy of grace, and set apart in a place of quiet,—the friend of grace. Besides, the Friars by words of charitable exhortation and by the example of holy conversation incite and induce him to good. But the grace which one hath in the world is easily lost and retained with difficulty.[10] For the care of worldly affairs, the mother of confusion and bitterness, hindereth and disturbeth the sweetness of grace, nor can they live peacefully together. Other worldlings, too, by ruinous counsel and by the example of most wicked living withdraw him from good and impel him to evil, as it were, with violence. For they help not one behaving aright, but mock him. They do not oppose the enemies of God, but extol them. Wherefore it is better to possess one grace only in security than ten in such peril and fear.

HERE END THE SAYINGS OF BROTHER GILES.

[10] This is the reading found in the "Chron. XXIV General.," p. 95. The codex reads "conversationis ipsum provocare et accenditur et difficile conservatur." See Ed. No. 83.

VI

THREE NOTABLE SAYINGS[1]

TO one asking why evils grow up in man rather than good things, he replied: "Since the malediction the earth is more prone to bring forth bad herbs than good ones; however, the constant laborer can labor so continuously that the bad herbs shall hardly be able to increase."

In like manner he said of predestination that the seashore was sufficient for him to wash his hands, feet, and whole body, and that he was foolish who asked about that which was in the depths of the sea; and he to whom the knowledge of doing good is sufficient, ought not seek too high things.

Being asked what he thought of the Blessed Francis, he replied, all aglow at the mention of Blessed Francis, saying: "That man Francis ought never to be named without a man smacking his lips for joy; only one thing was wanting to him: namely, bodily strength, for if he had had such a body as I have, that is to say, as robust, without doubt the whole world would never be able to follow him."

---

[1] From the "Liber de Conformit." See Ed., Nos. 69 and 70.

APPENDIX II

SOME ADDITIONAL SAYINGS (FROM THE ASSISI MSS. 403 AND 676)

THAT thou mayest attain what thou desirest, keep in thy heart, words, and works this teaching, for it is that of Brother Giles, the companion of the Blessed Francis.

Adapt all thy senses according to place and time; wherefore, if thou art interrogated, reply to edification; if asked to do something, help for the sake of merit and good example; if bound by a command, willingly fulfil it, because of the great good of obedience.

Moderate thyself in food and drink, because they war against the soul.

Foresee thy words so that they may come to the palate before they come to the tongue.[1]

Beware of unseemly laughter and jeering, because they do much to make man despised.

Beware of talkativeness, because he that useth many words hurteth his soul.[2]

Beware of lying, because it rendereth man disreputable.

Beware of deceitful words, because His communication was with the simple.[3]

---

[1] See "Speculum Monachorum" (P. L., 184, 1176). See also St. Bonav., "Opera Omnia," t. viii, p. 485, n. 5.

[2] See Eccli. 20 : 8.

[3] Prov. 3 : 32.

Let thy words be few and useful and thoughtful.

If it happeneth and if it be necessary that thou do a service for any one, strive quickly to return to thine own duty. Return with haste from the body to the soul.

For the sake of a quiet conscience, despise no one.

Strive to perform in thyself and imitate every good work and good example by which man is commended by God and men, and on the other hand hate and abominate bad example and evil work, which render man despicable before God and men.

Praise not thyself and thine own, for this is blameworthy.

Reveal not the secrets of the heart, for this is what the foolish do.

Contend not, for this cannot be without sin.

Despise not, lest thou fall into some misfortune.

Contradict not thy elder, but without contention and murmuring seek humbly to obey, and presume not to do anything without obedience.

Blame no one unless thou see him sin.

Be moved to pity when thou hearest or seest any one sin, and praise God because He hath delivered thee from a like occasion, and for that reason unite thyself more to the sinner.

Flee from knowing the sins of others, for charity hath its reward.

Appendix II

Often examine thy standing, whether thou art in a good state or the contrary.

Beware, with the greatest care, of the glance of men or women, parents or friends, servants, and also of rational and irrational creatures, because they cause a certain curiosity and they thus remove sincerity of heart.

In like manner close thy ears and lips to murmuring, detraction, backbiting, and whatever thou hearest relish not, and care not to hear save God.

"With all watchfulness keep thy heart,"[4] that thou mayest think of nothing and wish nothing, desire or love nothing, save eternal life, so that thou mayest say with the prophet: "One thing I have asked of the Lord," etc.[5]

Set aside and forget all things; first, thy parents, after the example of Christ who commended His Mother to John; secondly, honors, after the example of Christ who fled when they wished to make Him king; thirdly, effeminacies, after the example of Christ who was wrapped in mean clothes and laid in a manger; fourthly, worldly business, after the example of Christ who, having dismissed the crowd, went up into the mountain; fifthly, friendship and all familiarities, after the example of Christ who dwelt at intervals in desert places.

Love poor clothes, because they often beget humility in thy soul.

Love poverty, that thou mayest be able to imitate the Poor Christ, and that thou mayest the more freely give thyself to God.

[4] Prov. 4:23.   [5] Ps. 26:4.

Serve all carefully, for Christ came not to be ministered to, but to minister.

Carry nothing strange about with thee, for the heart wandereth much about such things.

Flee from useless rumors, for in the like things the will of man wavereth.

Strive to acquire purity of conscience, that thou mayest immediately feel what is opposed to thy soul; and that when thou feelest it, thou mayest at once say to the Lord, "Through my fault"; wherefore blessed is he that hath a reproving conscience, for if thou accusest thyself, the Lord will excuse thee. Strive also to confess humbly in those things of which thy conscience accuseth thee.

Go often to prayer daily, that if the Lord shall always visit thee when thou prayest it may be well; if He should not always visit thee, hope for Him and knock with tears and humble confession, saying: "Lord, I am a false religious, a proud hypocrite, vainglorious, ungrateful for Thy favors," etc.

The Lord gave sight to the man blind from his birth by spittle and clay.

Recall daily in the bitterness of thy soul at the ninth hour, or at any hour, the Passion of the Lord and the sins of thy neighbors. After Compline be careful to pray, and at the beginning of the watches rise and praise the Lord. At midnight and after Matins, seek a quiet time for prayer, after the example of Christ who passed the night in prayer in desert places.

Flee from all those who gainsay thy combat.

Appendix II

Be silent in so far as thou canst, so that thou speak not much with any one, save with those who can help thee in thy combat.

Rest in eternal life by lifting thyself above thyself, thinking also of the Lord Jesus Christ and Him crucified, Almighty, All-Knowing, reigning everywhere.

Think of the heavenly country, the choirs of angels, the helping angel, and the tempting angel.

Descend into the depths; consider the pains of hell; think in bitterness of thy sins.

O Holy Poverty, those who imitate and love thee, to them thou art the ark of the heavenly King.

O Lady Humility, those who have found and guarded thee will have a good gift.

O Lady Chastity, thou art so fair and frail that the foolish find thee not, nor can they possess thee.

O Holy and Good Will, to him who knoweth how to guard thee, thou wilt be the way to a heavenly reward.

O Holy Resolution, to those who know how to keep thee, thou wilt be the way of every good.

O Lady Patience, how beautiful thou art, for thou art the daughter of the King of heaven and earth.

O Lady Devotion, thou art so profitable that thou adornest the soul in many ways.

O Lady Honesty, what a garden thou art in which there are all things that give much delight.

O Lady Quail, I desire to come to thee to listen to the praises of God. I desire to remember that thou dost not say, "la la" (There, there!), but thou sayest "qua qua" (Here, here!).[6]

O Sister Dove, what a sweet plaint thou knowest how to make. Oh, sinner! what wilt thou do, since thou dost not wish to learn it?

Four things happened to the angels who were unwilling to persevere: hatred, on account of love; ugliness, on account of beauty; ruin, on account of security; punishment, on account of blessedness.

Turn and return, above and below, on one side and on the other, and nothing is left save to fight against the flesh which seeketh day and night to betray thee, and doth not rest; which if thou shalt have conquered and trampled under foot, thou wilt find every good at hand and no evil will be able to harm thee.[7]

I would more willingly hold one command in reverence, even though I did not understand it, than know how to explain one hundred commands without reverence and devotion.

If thou wouldst find grace, be discerning, reverent, and amiable, frank, and sweet.

It is so great a virtue to permit oneself to be lorded over by all, that we are not worthy to name it, but let us hold it in reverence.

---

[6] See "Chron. XXIV General.," p. 86.
[7] See above, p. 31; and "Chron. XXIV General.," p. 88.

Interior of S. Lorenzo, Perugia

Appendix II

The more any one inclineth his head the greater grace shall he find.

The Lord doth not wish men save unprofitable ones; wherefore, when thou hast done all things well, say: "We are unprofitable servants."[8]

If a king were to send his daughter to a certain place, would he put her on a wild, proud, and stubborn horse, and not rather on one that is meek and goeth easily? The king's daughter is Grace, which He will not give to the proud but to the humble.[9]

The more thou hast searched, so much the more thou wilt find; and the less thou searchest, so much the less.

It is impossible for him to come to good who hateth not evil.

To know how to bear injuries is the way of holy men and women and not of others.

What thou art in suffering, such art thou in the sight of God.

A certain Brother said to him that the Brothers made him work so hard that he could hardly stand up at prayer, and therefore he begged for an obedience to go to a hermitage. To whom he replied: "If thou goest to the King of France, and bendest thy knee before him and sayest: 'Lord, give me a thousand marks,' would he not reply: 'Fool, what hast thou done for me that I should give thee a thousand marks?' But if beforehand thou hadst done him a great

[8] Luke 17: 10.   [9] See above, p. 14.

service, he would not allow thee to seek the favor long." [10]

It is a greater virtue to do one thing according to the will of another than two according to one's own will.

A certain Brother said to him that at times he strove hard to find grace and could not. To whom he said: " Confess thy fault, for He who hath all in His power can give on one day what He doth not give on another. Hence there is nothing left save that thou servest faithfully."

If a man had lived from Adam even till the the end of the world, and had done all the good he could, he would not merit the least condescension from God.

The man who fleeth temptation fleeth from eternal life, according to the words "He is not crowned except he strive lawfully." [11]

If the whole world were full of men up to the clouds and only one were to be saved, yet each one ought to strive to follow up his grace so that he might be that one.[12]

A certain person asked how he might become spiritual. Who (Giles) said: " Look at that field which is more fertile than the other which is next it. Why is it thus? Because the owner of this toiled more than the owner of that field which is barren. And the smith

---

[10] See "Chron. XXIV General.," p. 87; also Ed., No. 78.

[11] II Tim. 2 : 5. See "Chron. XXIV General.," p. 87, and Ed., No. 79.

[12] See above, p. 44.

Appendix II

striketh the iron with many blows that it may be brought to perfection." [13]

It is impossible for the devil to enter where love abideth.

The devil fleeth from the creature for nothing else than for love. Wherefore a man ought not to rest until he loveth.

Any one who honoreth others can hardly ever fall grievously.

With toil upon toil strive after kindness. I know not whether under heaven there be greater wisdom than this.

A certain person had no eyes or hands or feet. Some one said to him: "If anybody were to restore thee feet, what wouldst thou give him?" He answered: "A hundred pounds." "And if some one were to restore thee hands?" He replied: "All my goods." "And if one were to give light to thine eyes?" He replied: "I would serve him all the days of my life." Behold the Lord hath given thee feet and hands and eyes, and all things corporal and spiritual, and thou wilt not serve him." [14]

If thou workest the good which thou knowest, thou shalt come to the good which thou knowest not.

Works are farther away from our strength than heaven is from the earth.

If some one were to give thee permission to enter a vineyard and help thyself to the

---

[13] See above, p. 43; also "Chron. XXIV General.," p. 87.

[14] See "Chron. XXIV General.," p. 87, and Ed., No. 78.

grapes at will, would the leaves, thinkest thou, stand in thy way?

It is a thousand times better that man should teach himself than teach the whole world.

If thou wilt know much, labor much and bow thy head much.

A noble preacher is Lady Humility, Lady Patience.

What is humility? Give each his due.

A man should not speak too pompously, nor too uncouthly, but ordinarily.

The bleating sheep is a long way off from the one that is eating.[15]

It is one kind of humility to give place to God, another to consider thyself in very truth as thou art.

This world is a field of such sort that he who possesseth the most possesseth the worst part.[16]

The world is most horrible for the wicked, most admirable for the good.

Narrow is the way, namely, in the custody of the heart.

If one were in the midst of many enemies who were hurling darts and arrows and stones at him, it would do him no good to lay down his arms.

---

[15] This and the eight preceding paragraphs are found in the " Chron. XXIV General.," p. 85, under the heading "How he admonished the lazy Brothers preaching willingly to others."

[16] See above, p. 29.

Appendix II

The portions of food are ready, but there is none to receive.[17]

I wish to have such a master that if I should be in the convent, he might be with me; if in a hermitage, likewise; if in the market-place or the forest, likewise.

Even as a good habit is the way to all good, so is a bad habit to all evil.[18]

[17] See " Chron. XXIV General.," p. 87.
[18] See above, p. 66.

BIBLIOGRAPHY

BIBLIOGRAPHY

IN the preparation of the present volume I have tried to study everything, old and new, within reach, dealing with Blessed Giles. For the benefit of those who may be interested in this subject I herewith append a list of the principal works I have cited or referred to as authorities, adding here and there a few words of explanation as to the character of those less known to the general reader. I have thought it better to omit references to works not easily accessible. The critical student of Franciscan sources will know where to find such works better than I can tell him.

ACTA SANCTORUM. This celebrated collection, started about the middle of the seventeenth century under the direction of Father John Bollandus, and continued by other Fathers of the Society of Jesus known as the Bollandists, contains the "Historia Vitae B. Aegidii," edited, after a Perugian MS. now lost, by Papebroche, who contributes a valuable "Commentarius Praevius" and notes. This Life is followed by a lengthy collection of the "Dicta Aurea" and a list of miracles wrought through Blessed Giles's intercession after his death. See "Acta SS.," April, t. iii, edit. noviss., 1866, pp. 222-249.

ACTUS B. FRANCISCI ET SOCIORUM EJUS. This work, in 8vo, pp. lxiv-272, which dates from

c. 1270-1328, was edited by M. Paul Sabatier in 1902. It forms vol. iv of the "Collection d'Etudes" and comprises with other matter the Latin text of the traditional "Fioretti." Chapters 44, 45, 46, and 47 have special reference to Blessed Giles. The delicate question of the Leonine biography is treated in the Introduction. See "Actus B. Francisci," p. lviii, and passim. There is a copious index.

ANALECTA BOLLANDIANA. A quarterly review of hagiographical literature published at Brussels by the Bollandists. Most of the articles on Franciscan subjects are from the pen of Fr. Francis Van Ortroy, S.J. On the "Vita" and "Dicta B. Aegidii," see tt. vi (1887), p. 171; xvii (1898), p. 380; xix (1900), p. 72; xxi (1902), p. 112, and xxiv (1905), p. 410.

ANALECTA FRANCISCANA. The series published under this title by the Friars Minor at St. Bonaventure's College, Quaracchi, contains the texts of a number of early chronicles of the Franciscan Order. Three volumes have appeared so far. Vol. iii, issued in 1897 (in 4to, pp. xxviii-748), contains the well-known "Chronica XXIV Generalium" (referred to herein as "Chron. XXIV General."), a compilation dating from c. 1369-1374 and including many early documents, notably a "Vita Fratris Aegidii," which no less a critic than Papini regarded as the genuine Leonine biography. The editing of this chronicle was done in greatest part by Fr. Quinctianus Müller, O.F.M. See t. iii, pp. 77-115, and passim.

Bartholomew, Fr., of Pisa, O.F.M.: DE CONFORMITATE VITAE B. FRANCISCI AD VITAM D. N. JESU CHRISTI. This remarkable work, which has been condemned with most unmerited ostracism by those who have not had the patience to study it, was begun about 1385, and approved by the General Chapter of the Friars Minor held in 1399. A critical edition of the text, which is sorely needed, will appear in vol. iv of the "Analecta Franciscana." Meanwhile my references are to the edition printed at Milan in 1510. It contains excerpts from the life of Giles and a collection of his "Sayings." See Pis. viii, P. ii, fol. liii a ff.

Bernard, Fr., of Besse, O.F.M.: LIBER DE LAUDIBUS B. FRANCISCI. In this short legend, which was published in 1897, both at Quaracchi ("Anal. Francis.," t. iii, pp. 666-692.), and by Fr. Hilarin Felder of Lucerne, O. M. Cap. (Rome, ex typ. Editrice Industriale), Bernard of Besse, who lived about 1278 and was secretary to St. Bonaventure, makes interesting mention of Giles (c. 1.). Father Hilarin's edition also includes a valuable reference to the fragmentary life of Giles contained in the Freiburg MS., 23 J. 60.

S. Bonaventure: LEGENDAE DUAE DE VITA S. FRANCISCI. Quaracchi, 1898, in 16mo, pp. viii-270. In chap. 3, n. 4, of the "Legenda Major," the Seraphic Doctor bears important witness to the virtues and ecstasies of Giles. There is an English translation of this work by Miss Lockhart, 4th edit., 1898. London: Washbourne.

S. Bonaventure: OPERA OMNIA. Quaracchi, 1882-1902, in 4to maj. Vol. xi. There is a special reference made to Giles not only in the "Legenda Major" of St. Bonaventure, c. 3, but also in the Commentary on St. Luke, Sermon for Holy Saturday, and elsewhere. See "Opera Omnia," t. vii, p. 231, t. ix, 269, etc.

Briganti, Mgr. Antonio: IL BEATO EGIDIO D'ASSISI. Monografia. Napoli, M. d'Auria, 1898, in 16mo, pp. xii-356. An edifying biography. See "Anal. Bolland.," t. xix, p. 72, and "Miscell. Frances.," vol. vii, fasc. iv, p. 137.

BULLETTINO CRITICO DI COSE FRANCESCANE. A quarterly review published at Florence, Presso il libraio Francesco Lumachi, under the auspices of Luigi Suttina. Contains, I, 41, an article by the late Count Manzoni, "Alcuni Capitoli in volgare inediti di Frate Egidio, terzo compagno di S. Francesco."

Carmichael, Montgomery: See "Downside Review," and "Franciscan Annals."

Celano, Fr. Thomas de: LEGENDA PRIMA B. FRANCISCI. The story of Giles's conversion is recorded in this work, which forms, so to say, the cornerstone of Franciscan history. See I Cel., § 25, also § 30, in the definitive edition of Celano's "Lives," by Père Edouard d'Alençon: "S. Francisci Assisiensis vita et miracula, additis opusculis liturgicis, auctore Fr. Thoma de Celano. Hanc editionem novam ad fidem MSS. recensuit P. Eduardus Alenconiensis O. F. M. Cap." Rome, Desclée, 1906, in 16mo, pp. lxxxvii–481.

COLLECTION D'ETUDES ET DE DOCUMENTS SUR L'HISTOIRE RELIGIEUSE ET LITTERAIRE DU MOYEN AGE. In this series, published in 8vo in Paris by the Librairie Fischbacher, several of the early MS. collections referred to in the present volume are described in detail. See Index to tt. i, ii, and iv. V. Manuscrits.

Cristofani Antonio, DELLE STORIE D'ASSISI, libri sei. 2 ed., Assisi, 1875, 2 vols. in 8vo.

CHRONICA XXIV GENERALIUM. See under "Analecta Franciscana."

De Kerval, L.: SAINT FRANÇOIS D'ASSISE ET L'ORDRE SERAPHIQUE. Vanves, 1898. See pp. 412-414, on the importance of Giles's life and teaching for a right understanding of early Franciscan history.

DICTA BEATI AEGIDII ASSISIENSIS, sec. codices MSS. emendata et denuo edita a PP. Collegii S. Bonaventurae ad Claras Aquas (Quaracchi, 1905, in 16mo., pp. xx-124). This, the first critical edition of the Latin text of Giles's "Sayings," has been described above (see p. lx). They miss much who do not read these "Sayings" in the original.

DOCUMENTA ANTIQUA FRANCISCANA, edidit Fr. Leonardus Lemmens, O.F.M. Pars i: Scripta Fratris Leonis socii S. P. Francisci. Ad Claras Aquas, Quaracchi, 1901, in 16mo, pp. 106. This volume contains (see pp. 37-63) the short life of Giles attributed to Brother Leo after MS. 1/63 of St. Isidore's College, Rome (see above, p. x). In part iii of the same series (Quaracchi, 1902, pp. 6-12) will be found Fr. Lemmens's comments on the criticisms passed upon this life by Fr. Van Ortroy and others.

DOWNSIDE REVIEW for April 1902 contains (pp. 1-17) an article by Mr. Montgomery Carmichael, entitled "The First Franciscan Convent," which is valuable in connection with the controverted question as to whether Giles was received by St. Francis at Rivotorto or at the Porziuncula. See also under "Franciscan Annals."

Dubois, Leo L., S.M.: SAINT FRANCIS OF ASSISI: SOCIAL REFORMER. New York, Benziger Brothers. 1906. See p. 230.

Edouard, Fr., d'Alençon. See under "Celano."

Felder, Fr. Hilarin, O.M. Cap.: GESCHICHTE DER WISSENSCHAFTLICHEN STUDIEN IM FRANCISKANERORDEN BIS UM DIE MITTE DES 13. JAHRHUNDERTS. Von P. Dr. Hilarin Felder, O. Cap., Lektor der Heiligen Theologie. Freiburg und St. Louis, Mo., B. Herder, 1904, in 8vo, pp. xi-557. This weighty volume, which deals with the development of studies in the first century of the Order, must appeal to all interested in the question of Franciscan origins, even though — like myself — they are unable to accept all the conclusions of its learned author. In so far as Giles is concerned, see pp. 34 and 64; also for further references, pp. 177 and 234.

FIORETTI DI SAN FRANCESCO should if possible be read in Italian. Perhaps the best version hitherto published for the general reader is Antonio Cesari's (Verona, 1822), based on the epoch-making edition of Filippo Buonarroti (Florence, 1718). The Crusca quote from both these editions. For a list of translations containing selections from the "Dicta," see above, p. lvii.

FRANCISCAN ANNALS. Crawley. October, 1906. See "The Date of the Foundation of the Order," by Montgomery Carmichael. It is a help toward determining the time of Giles's reception by St. Francis.

FRANCISCAN MONTHLY. London, 1906. A series (January to June) of articles on Giles.

Fratini, M. Conv., Fr. Guiseppe: VITA DEL B. EGIDIO D'ASSISI. Assisi, Tip. Metastasio, 1898, in 16mo, pp. xvi-144. This biography is satisfactory so far as it goes, but it should not be read with a critical eye. See "Anal. Bolland.," t. xvii, p. 380, and "Misc. Frances.," vol. vii, fasc. i, p. 30.

Goetz, Prof. Walter: DIE QUELLEN ZUR GESCHICHTE DES HL. FRANZ VON ASSISI. Gotha, Perthes, 1904. On the question of the Leonine Life of Giles, see p. 98.

Golubovich, O.F.M., Fr. Girolamo: BIBLIOTECA BIO-BIBLIOGRAFICA DELLA TERRA SANTA E DELL' ORIENTE FRANCESCANO, t. i (1215-1300), Quaracchi, 1906, in 8vo, pp. viii-479. This thoroughly critical work is a veritable mine of information, not only as regards the rôle played by the first Franciscans in the Orient, but also concerning the early history of the whole Order. For the story of Giles's visit to the Holy Places and to Tunis, and for the general chronology of his life, see pp. 105, 91, 47, 52, 60, 85, 103, 116.

Lemmens, O.F.M., Fr. Leonard: FRAGMENTA MINORA. CATALOGUS S. FRATRUM MINORUM. Quem scriptum circa 1335 edidit notisque illustravit Fr. Leonardus Lemmens. Romae: typis Sallustianis, 1903, in 8vo, pp. xvi-54. In this anonymous work, which dates from the year 1335, Giles is referred to in almost the same words as in the " Liber de Laudibus." See p. 8.

Le Monnier, Leon: HISTOIRE DE ST. FRANÇOIS D'ASSISE. Paris, Lecoffre. 1889. Two vols. An English translation of this excellent biography was published in 1894. London, Kegan Paul.

Bibliography

Little, A. G.: INITIA OPERUM LATINORUM quae saeculis xiii, xiv, xv, attribuuntur. Manchester University Press, 1904, in 8vo, pp. xii–275. This work is a valuable help to any one compiling a catalogue of Franciscan MSS. Professor Little's description of Codex 525 of the Bodleian Library, Oxford, which appeared in the "Opuscules de Critique historique," t. i., p. 247 ff, has been used in the present work.

LIVES OF THE SAINTS AND BLESSED OF THE THREE ORDERS OF ST. FRANCIS. Vol. ii of this excellent work, which is translated from the "Auréole Seraphique" of Père Leon, O.F.M., and published by the Franciscan Convent at Taunton, contains (pp. 89-100) a brief but comprehensive biographical sketch of Blessed Giles.

Macdonell, Anne: SONS OF ST. FRANCIS. London, Dent. 1902, in 16mo, pp. 436. The clever and suggestive sketch of Blessed Giles included in this volume (pp.51–79) is discolored owing to the professed bias of the authoress. See p. 3.

Menge, O.F.M., Fr. Gisbert: DER SELIGE AEGIDIUS VON ASSISI. Sein Leben und seine Sprüche. Paderborn: Junfermann, 1906, in 12mo, pp. xvi–118. This unpretending volume contains, besides a German version of the "Dicta," a summary of the life and miracles of Giles, based on the "Chron. XXIV General." and "Acta SS." It is the work of a thoroughly devout scholar.

MISCELLANEA FRANCESCANA. This valuable periodical, published at Foligno under the auspices of Mgr. Faloci-Pulignani, may be said to represent the extreme conservative view of things Franciscan. During the twenty years that have elapsed since its foundation, various aspects of the Life and Sayings of Blessed Giles have been treated in its pages. See in particular, vol. iv, fasc. v. p. 157; vol. vii, fasc. i, p. 30, and iv, p. 137; vol. ix, fasc. iii, p. 76.

MONUMENTA GERMANIAE HISTORICA. See under Salimbene.

ŒUVRES DE S. FRANÇOIS D'ASSISE. Translation of Berthaumier (Paris, Poussielgue, 1863) in 12mo. Following the works of St. Francis, this volume contains a good, though incomplete, version of the *Dicta*. A new French translation of the latter is announced for early publication — besides Italian and Spanish ones.

OPUSCULES DE CRITIQUE HISTORIQUE. In this series, published in 8vo, by A. Ducros, Valence, descriptions of the Leignitz, Oxford, and Budapest MSS. (herein referred to as containing the "Dicta") by M. Sabatier, Prof. Little, and Prof. Katona, respectively, have appeared. See fasc. ii, v, and ix.

OPUSCULA SANCTI PATRIS FRANCISCI ASSISIENSIS. Quaracchi, 1904, in 16mo, pp. xvi-209. This, the first critical edition of the Latin works of St. Francis, has been translated into English by the present writer. See the "Writings of St. Francis of Assisi," Philadelphia, The Dolphin Press. 1906, in 8vo, pp. xxxii-208. See pp. 137 and 187.

ORIENTE SERAFICO. See under Patrem.

Panfilo, Fr., da Magliano, O.F.M.: STORIA COMPENDIOSA DI S. FRANCESCO E DEI FRANCESCANI, Rome, 1874-76, two vols., in 18mo. It is a matter for regret that Fr. Panfilo did not live to complete this excellent compendium. So far as it goes, however, it is thoroughly reliable.

Papini, M. Conv., Fr. Nicholas: LA STORIA DI S. FRANCESCO D'ASSISI, Opera critica. Foligno, 1827, 2 vols. in 4to. See l. 2, p. 212; also "Notizie sicure sopra S. Francesco e invenzione del suo santo corpo," 2 edit., Foligno, 1824, p. 126. Even though one may be out of sympathy with the point of view of the severely critical author of these works, no one interested in our present subject can afford to overlook them.

Patrem, O.F.M., Fr. Leon: APPUNTI CRITICI SULLA CRONOLOGIA DELLA VITA DI S.

FRANCESCO. These splendid chronological studies appeared in the "Oriente Serafico," Assisi, 1895, an. vii, n. 4 ff., and have been reprinted in the " Misc. Frances.", vol. ix, fasc. iii. They richly deserve an English translation.

Salimbene, O.F.M., Fr.: CHRONICON. My references to this famous chronicle, one of the most remarkable human documents of the thirteenth century, are to the imperfect edition published at Parma in 1857. A critical edition of the complete text is being published in the " Monumenta Germaniae Historica," by Prof. Holder-Egger. Vol. xxvii, pars. i, contains the first 176 pages of the Parma edition, besides the "Liber de Prelato," pp. 410-414; the second part will, it is hoped, appear in 1907.

Salter, Emma Gurney: FRANCISCAN LEGENDS IN ITALIAN ART. Dent, 1905. It is a matter of regret that the Gozzoli medallion of Giles has not been reproduced in this valuable work. For reference to it see p. 161.

Sbaralea, O.M. Conv., Fr. Hyacinth: SUPPLEMENTUM ET CASTIGATIO AD SCRIPTORES TRIUM ORDINUM S. FRANCISCI A WADDINGO ALIISVE DESCRIPTOS. Opus posthumum. Rome, 1806. A list of different editions of the " Dicta " is given on p. 4.

SCRIPTA FRATRIS LEONIS. See under "Doc. Ant. Francis."

SOME PAGES OF FRANCISCAN HISTORY. Under this title two articles, on the Sources of Franciscan literature and the controversies concerning them, which appeared in "The Dolphin" for July and August, 1905, have been reprinted by the London Catholic Truth Society.

SPECULUM PERFECTIONIS. Edit. Sabatier, 1898. In the critical Introduction which forms not the least valuable portion of this volume, many references to the Life and "Sayings" of Giles occur. See Index, under " Aegidius."

Symonds, Margaret, and Lina Duff Gordon: THE STORY OF PERUGIA (Medieval Towns Series), Dent, 1898. On the Convent of S. Francesco al Monte, where Giles died, see pp. 197 ff. See also p. 237.

TRIUM SOCIORUM, LEGENDA S. FRANCISCI ASSIS. Ed. Faloci. Foligno, 1898. English translation by E. Gurney Salter: "The Legend of the Three Companions." Dent, 1902. Chap. ix contains the story of Giles's vocation and of his journey to the Marches with St. Francis.

Wadding, O.F.M., Fr. Luke: ANNALES MINORUM, vol. iv (Rome, 1732) of this monumental collection, ad annum 1262, contains an excellent compendium of the life of Giles, together with a selection from his "Sayings." See also Wadding's "Scriptores Ordinis Minorum" (Rome, 1650), p. 5 for a succinct characterization of the "Sayings."

For further bibliographical references see Chevalier; "Répertoire des Sources Historiques du Moyen Age" (Paris, Librairie de la Société Bibliographique, 1877-1886), p. 877; "Bibliotheca Hagiographica Latina antiquae et mediae aetatis" (ed. Soc. Bolland., Brussels, 1898-1901), pp. 16-17; and 1308; Hurter, "Nomenclatur Literarius Cath." (ed. iii, 1906, Oeniponte) t. ii, p. 375.

INDEX

A

Abbreviations used in citing MSS., lxi n
"Acta Sanctorum," xi n, xxxv n, xlii n, liii n, lvi, 11 n. See also Bollandists and "Analecta Bollandiana"
Active Life, Giles on the, 49
"Actus B. Francisci et Sociorum ejus," xii
Aegidius. See Giles
Africa, xxv
Agello, xxi
Albert of Pisa, xlvi
Alexander of Hales, xxviii
Alger. Abby Langdon, lviii n
"Analecta Bollandiana," vii n, viii, 1 n, li n. See also Bollandists and Van Ortroy
"Analecta Franciscana," x n, xv n, xvi n, xxii n, xxviii n, xxx n, xxxix n, xl n, li n, lvi n, 74
Ancona, xxi. See also Marches
Andrew of Burgundy, companion of Giles, xxx, li, 66 n
Angelico, Fra, xlv n
Angelo, Porta S. See Perugia

Angelus a S. Francisco, Fr., lix
"Annales Minorum" quoted, xii, xv, xx n, xxi n, xxiv n, xxv n, xxx n, xxxviii n, xl n, xlii n, lvi n. See also Wadding
"Annales typographici," lvi n, lvii n
Antoninus, St., lvi
Antwerp, lv
Appiani, F., xlv
"Appunti critici." See Patrem
Arnold of Sarano, Fr., x n
Arnold, T. W., lviii n
Asceticism, Early Franciscan school of, the characteristics of, vii
Assisi, xiii, xxvii, xli, 96. See also Church

B

Bari, xxii
Bartholomew of Pisa, xii, xxi n, xxvi n, liii, lvi, 23 n, 33 n, 36 n, 45 n, 46 n, 68 n, 70 n, 71 n, 72 n, 73 n, 74 n, 91 n, 93 n, 94 n, 95 n, 106 n
Bastia, xli, xliii n
Belcari, Feo, lvii
Benincasa, xxv
Benozzo Gozzoli, his medallion of Giles, xlvi

Bernard of Quintavalle, xii, xiii, xiv, xvi, xxvi, xxxi, 44 n, 96
"Biblioteca della Terra Santa." See Golubovich
"Bibliotheca Franciscana ascetica," lx
"Bibliotheca Hagiographa Latina," lv n
Biographers, Giles's, ancient and modern, viii, ix, x, xi, xii
Bollandiana. See "Analecta"
Bollandists, vii, xi, xxvi n, xxxv, xlii, lii, liii, lvi, 76 n. See also "Acta Sanctorum," "Analecta Bollandiana," and Van Ortroy
Bonaventure, St., quoted, xii, xvii, xx n, xxix n, xlvi, l, 20 n, 46 n; interview with Giles, xxix
Bracci, Fr. Alessio, lxiii
Breviary, Franciscan, xv n, xlii n
Briganti, Mgr., his biography of Giles, viii
Brindisi, xxi
Brussels, lvi
Buonarroti, F., lvii n

C

Canonization of certain Friars, Giles on, 74
Carceri, the, xliv
Carmichael, Montgomery, quoted, xv, xvi n, xvii, lxiii, 94 n
"Catalogus Librorum Impressorum," lv n

"Catalogus Sanctorum Fratrum Minorum," xli n
Catana, Peter of. See Peter
Celano, Thomas of, quoted, xii n, xiii, xvii, 11 n
Cetona, xxx, xxxi, xxxiii
Chansons de geste, 61 n
Chapter, Second General, xxv
Charlemagne, 61 n
Chastity, Giles on holy, 30
Chiara, S. See Church
Chiusi, xxx
"Chronica Parmensis." See Salimbene
"Chronica XXIV Generalium," ix, x, xi, xii, xiv n, xvi, xxi n, xliii n, lv, 6 n, 7 n, 25 n, 30 n, 33 n, 35 n, 36 n, 38 n, 39 n, 41 n, 43 n, 44 n, 46 n, 50 n, 64 n, 66 n, 73 n, 83 n, 91 n, 105 n, 112 n, 114 n, 115 n, 116 n, 117 n
Chronologies of Giles's life, difficulties in, xviii
Church of St. Chiara, Assisi, xii; S. Francesco a Ripa, Rome, xxii n; S. Francesco al Prato, Perugia, xli, xliii; S. Giorgio, Assisi, xiii; S. Lorenzo, Cathedral of, Perugia, xliii; S. Lorenzo, Deruta, xxiv; S. Onofrio, chapel in S. Lorenzo, xlii; S. Rufino, Assisi, xiii
Clare, St., xxviii, 11 n
Collection d'Etudes, lx n
Collections of Dicta. See Sayings
Colle d'Inferno, xxvii

Index

Cologne, lv
Combat with Temptation, Giles on, 34
Companions, the Three, xxv n, li n. See also Bernard, Giles, Leo, etc.
Compostella. See St. James
Conformities, Book of. See Bartholomew of Pisa
Conrad of Offida, Blessed, xli, xliii
Contemplation, Giles on, 46
Contempt of the World, Giles on, 28
Contrition, Giles on, 97
Controversy as to date and place of Giles's Reception by St. Francis, xiv, xvii; as to observance of Rule, xxvii
Conventuals, lxiii
Coppoli, James of, gives house on Monteripido to Franciscans, xliv
Correspondence with Grace, Giles on, 73
Crescentius of Gesi, xxvi n, xlvi
Crispolti, Chapel of the, xlii
Cristofani, historian, quoted, xiii n

D

Dante, quoted, xii
Deruta, xxiv
De Selincourt, Mrs., xlv n
Dicta. See Sayings
Di Salvo, Marchesa, lviii n
"Documenta Antiqua Franciscana," x n, xi n, xvi n, xvii n, li n, lii n, 91 n, 94 n

Donovan, Fr. Stephen, lxiii
Douai, lix
"Downside Review," xvi n
Du Cange, 26 n, 61 n

E

Editions of the Golden Sayings: Antwerp, lv; Bologna, lv; Brussels, lvi; Cologne, lv; Mentz, lv; Quaracchi, lx; Salamanca, lvi
Edouard d'Alençon, P., xii n, xxxviii n
Egidio. See Giles
Elias erects collection box at Assisi, xxvii; his excommunication, xvii, xlvi
"Etudes Franciscaines," li n, lvi n
Eubel, Conrad, xxvi n

F

Fabriano, xxvi, xxx
Fabriano, Luigi da, xxvi n
Fac Secundum Exemplar, liii, lxi
Faith, Giles on, 6
Faloci Pulignani, Mgr., xii n. See under Trium Sociorum
Fear of the Lord, Giles on, 15, 81
Felder, Fr. Hilarius, xxviii n
Fidelis of Fauna, Fr., lx n
"Fioretti," The, xii n, xxxiii, xxxvi, lvii, lix; translations of, containing Dicta lviii, lix. See also "Actus B. Francisci," and "Floretum"

Florence, xlv n
"Floretum S. Francisci," xxxiii n
Foschi, Mgr., Archbishop of Perugia, xliii
Francesco, S. See Church
Francis, St.: calls Giles the Knight of his Round Table, vii; receives him to a share in his poverty, xiii; takes him as companion in journey to the Marches, testimony of, quoted, xxi n; acquires Convent of S. Francesco a Ripa, xxii n; decides to send his Friars to evangelize the nations, xxv; assigns Giles to labor in Africa, xxv; gives him liberty to go where he pleases, xxvi; sends him to hermitage of Fabriano, xxvi; Giles present at death of, xxvi; appears to Giles at Cetona, xxx; attempts of Perugians to have him die in their city, xli; his picture by Benozzo Gozzoli, xlvi; he handed torch on to Giles, xlvii; "Writings" of, l n; opened sources from which he had drawn to his disciples, 61 n; Giles's estimate of him, 106
"Franciscan Annals," xv n, xviii n
Franciscan, Early, School of Asceticism, vii
Franciscan Legends in Italian Art, xlvi n

"Franciscan Monthly," 94 n
Fratini, Giuseppe, his biography of Giles, viii
Frederic, Emperor, 76 n
Friars Minor, Order of, Giles on, 62
Friars Minor, Origin of the name, 94
Fullerton, Lady Giorgiana, lviii n

G

Gerard, or Gerardino of San Donnino, xxxviii, xxxix
Geschichte, etc. See Felder and Goetz
Giles, Blessed, one of the First Companions of St. Francis, vii; Knight of the Franciscan Round Table, vii; ideal type of the Franciscan Friar, vii; biographies of, by Fratini, Briganti, Menge, viii; early lives of, x, xi, xii; story of his conversion and vocation, xiii, xiv; date and place of his reception by St. Francis, xiv, xvi, also 95 n; his parentage and early life unknown, xvii; difficulties in chronology of his life in the Order, xviii; his journey to the Marches with St. Francis, xix; accompanies St. Francis to Rome and there receives the ecclesiastical tonsure, xx; sets out for Spain, xx; visits Jerusalem, xxi; the first Franciscan to set foot in

Palestine, earns his food by manual labor in various ways, xxi, xxii; visits Monte Gargano and Bari, xxii; his method of life at Rome, xxii; always left time to recite Office, xxiii; his fervor at Holy Communion and reverence for ecclesiastical laws, xxiii; his simplicity when called a hypocrite by a priest, xxiii; his sojourn at Rieti with Cardinal Nicholas of Clairveaux, xxiv; retires to Deruta to pass Lent, xxiv; assigned by St. Francis to labor in Africa, xxv; failure of his mission in Tunis and return to Italy, xxv; asks St. Francis to assign him a convent, xxvi; is sent to hermitage at Fabriano, xxvi; is present at death of St. Francis and at that of Bernard of Quintavalle, xxvi; holds aloof from controversies as to observance of Rule, xvii; his conduct on learning of Elias's fall, xvii; visits the basilica at Assisi and rebukes the Friars for their disregard of poverty, xvii; preaches at St. Damian's before St. Clare, xxviii; inveighs against the schools of Paris as ruining the Order, xxviii; interview with St. Bonaventure, xxix; beginning of his ecstasies, xxx; tells of his four births, xxx; is favored with vision of St. Francis and afterwards of our Lord, xxx; ceases to go abroad, xxxi; his rejoinder to Bernard of Quintavalle, xxxi; is rapt before Gregory IX, xxxii; his advice to the Pope, xxxii; forcibly ejects an intruder from the convent garden, xxxiii; is visited by St. Louis, King of France, xxxiv; his frequent ecstasies and reputation as a speaker of "good words" draw many to see him, xxxvi; his answers to two Cardinals and to the Friars expelled from Sicily, xxxvii; and to a visionary and to one seeking spiritual counsel, xxxviii; quashes the arguments of Brother Gerardino with the help of a lute, xxxviii; gives strange advice to a would-be religious and to Brother Gratian, xxxix; no longer bewails his failure to obtain a martyr's crown, xl; desires to die of contemplation, xl; passes away peacefully, xl; date of his death, xl n; precautions of Perugians to retain his relics, xl; his answer to the Perugians and prediction regarding his canonization and miracles, xli; his remains after lying in state are transferred to the city and buried in marble sarcophagus, xli; tablet erected to his memory in chapel of the Crispolti, xlii; miracles wrought through his intercession recorded by Bollandists, xlii; his cultus confirmed by Pius VI, xlii; the only one of St. Francis's companions raised to honors of altar, xlii; translation of his remains to the archiepiscopal palace in 1860 and 1880, xliii; their present resting-place in the cathedral beside those of Bl. Conrad of Offida, xliii; his cell and garden on Monteripido, xliv; his grotto at the Carceri, xliv; scenes from his life painted on old table preserved at Pinacoteca, xliv; his medallion by Gozzoli at Montefalco is nearest approach to portrait, xlvi; he became a medium between the first and second generation of Friars, xlvi; is interrogated on all sides after St. Francis's death, xlvii; his "Golden Sayings"—their origin, collections, characteristics, etc., see "Sayings"; high authority of his spiritual teaching, xlix; not a theologian in narrow sense or even a lettered man, xlix; source of his knowledge, l; examples of his obedience, 64 n; how he settled sundry notable questions, 76; his estimate of St. Francis, 106

God, those in favor and disfavor with, Giles on, 86

Goetz, Walter, xi n

Golubovich, Girolamo, xxi n, xxv n, xl n, 83 n

Good Works, Giles on, 93

Gordon, Lina Duff. See Perugia

Graces acquired in Prayer, Story of Giles on, 71

Gratian, Brother, xxxix, li, 39 n

Gratitude, Giles on, 97

Gregory, ix, xxxii

Gregory, St., 72

H

Hagiography, Medieval, the methods of, xviii

Hain. See "Repertorium Biblicum"

Haymo of Faversham, xlvi

Holthrop. See "Catalogus"

Humility, Giles on, 12

Hurter, H., lv n

I

Incomprehensibility of God, Giles on, 6

Innocent III, xv, xx

J

Jacoba of Settesoli, Lady, xxxviii

Jacopone, Fra, of Todi, quoted, xxix

Jerusalem, Giles's visit to, xxi; establishment of Franciscans there, xxi n
John, Brother, companion of Giles, li
John of Parma, Blessed, xlvi
Jonas, sign of, Giles on, xli; story of, sculptured on his tomb, xli
Jongleurs, 11
Juniper Brother, 11 n, 30 n

K

Kaulen, Franz, lviii n
Knowledge useful and useless, Giles on, 53

L

Legenda Major. See Bonaventure
Legenda Trium Sociorum, ed. Civezza-Domenichelli, xv n; ed. Faloci, xii n, xvii, xx n
Lemmens, Fr. Leonard, x, xvii, xli n, lii, 91 n. See also "Catalogus," "Doc. Ant. Franc.," and "Scripta Fratris Leonis"
Le Monnier, Leon, quoted, xxxv n, xli n, 61 n
Leo, Brother, first biographer of Giles, ix; his attitude toward the abettors of laxity, xxvii; collection of Giles's "Sayings" attributed to him, li, lii
Leo XIII causes transfer of Giles's remains, xliii

Leonine life of Giles. See Leo
Littré Dict., 83 n
Lorenzo, S. See Church
Louis, Saint, King of France, visits Giles, xxxiii, xlv
Louis, Saint, of Toulouse, xxxvi
Love, Giles on, 9

M

Manning, Cardinal, lviii n
Manuscripts:—
  1. MSS. of Giles's life: Perugian, xi, xxvi n. "St. Isidore's 1/63," x, 91 n. See also Bibliography, under Bernard of Besse
  2. MSS. of Giles's "Sayings": different classes of, lii; different order in, liv n, lvi n; abbreviations used in citing, lxi n. "Assisi 121," 12 n, 22 n, 26 n, 36 n, 67 n. "Assisi 191," liv n. "Assisi 403," lv n, 107. "Assisi 590," liv n, 12 n, 26 n, 31 n, 36 n, 45 n, 50 n, 58 n, 68 n, 70 n, 71 n, 74 n, 97 n. "Assisi 676," lv n, 107. Bollandist MSS., lxi n, 11 n, 16 n, 18 n, 22 n, 23 n, 25 n, 33 n, 34 n, 36 n, 45 n, 47 n, 50 n, 52 n, 62 n, 65 n, 68 n, 70 n, 71 n, 72 n, 73 n, 74 n, 86 n, 91 n, 93 n, 94 n, 95 n, 100 n, 105 n, 108 n, 114 n, 115 n. Brussels, liv n. Buda Pest,

lii n, liii n. Deventer, liv n. Donaueschingen, lvii n. Florence Laurenziana, lii, liii, liv n, lxi, 12 n, 47 n, 52 n, 62 n, 65 n, 70 n, 71 n. Florence, National, lvii n. Hague, liv n. Liegnitz, lii n, liii n, 85 n. Leyden, lviii n. "Mentz 542," liv n; "Mentz 545," liv n. Munich, liv n. Oxford, lii n, liii n, 74 n, 75 n. Ravenna, lvii n. Rietberg, liv n, 50 n, 90 n. Rome Nat. Lib., lii n; Rome Ottob., lvii n. "Rome Vat. 4354," liii n, 12 n, 49 n, 52 n, 55 n, 62 n, 64 n, 68 n, 70 n, 82 n, 85 n. "Rome Vat. 9217," lvii n. "St. Isidore's 1/63," liii n, 12 n, 26 n, 44 n, 64 n, 68 n, 93 n. "St. Isidore's 1/73," lii n, liv n, 7 n, 12 n, 49 n, 52 n, 62 n, 64 n, 74 n, 82 n, 91 n. "St. Isidore's 1/82," 67 n. "St. Isidore's 1/83," liv n. "St. Isidore's 1/89," liii n, 94 n. Seville, lvii n. St. Florian, lii n. Utrecht liv n. Venice, lvii n. Vienna, lviii n. Vincenza, lvii n

Marches, Giles journey's with St. Francis to, xix, xxxi, xxxiii

Marco, S., Florence, xlv n

Mariotti, Candido, xx n

Mariotti, Carlo, xlv

Martha and Mary, Giles on, 22

Mason, Richard. See Angelus

Menge, Fr. Gisbert, his biography of Giles, viii, xv n, xl n, lviii n, lx n

Mentz, lv

"Miscellanea Francescana," viii n, xv n, xliv n

Mohammed, xxv

Montefalco, xiv

Montegargano, xxi

Monteripido, xxxvii, xl, xli, xliv

"Mornings in Florence." See Ruskin

Morocco, 74

Müller, Fr. Quinctianus, quoted, xv, xl n

Murillo, xxxii n

N

"Notizie Sicure." See Papini

O

Obedience and its utility, Giles on, 64

Onofrio, S. See Church

"Opuscula S. P. Francisci," lx. See also "Writings"

"Opuscules de Critique," lx n, 85

"Oriente Seraphico," xv n

P

Panfilo da Magliano, xv n

Panzer. See "Annales Typ."

Papebroche, xlii, lvi

Papini, O. M. Conv., Nich., viii, x, xv, xvii, xl n

"Paradiso." See Dante

Parenti, John, xlvi

Index

Patience, Giles on, 17
Patrem Leo, his chronological studies, xv n
Pecci, Cardinal. See Leo XIII
Penance, Giles on, 39
Perseverance, Giles on, 58
Perugia, xvii n, xxxii, xxxiv, xxxvi, xli, xliii, xliv, 91. See Churches, Story of, xxvi n, xliv n
Perugians, their desires for relics, xl; attempt to carry off St. Francis, xli; steal the body of Blessed Conrad, xli; tablet erected by them over Giles's tomb, xlii; give him the title of Blessed, xlii; decline in their devotion to him, xlii; reason for this decline, xliii
Peter of Catana, xiii, xiv, xvi, 96
Pinacoteca, Perugia, xliii, xliv
Poor Ladies, xxviii
Porziuncula, The, xvi, xvii, xviii, xxii n, xxv, xxvi, xxvii, xl, 95 n
Poverello. See under Francis
Prayer and its effect, Giles on, 40, 71; perseverance in, Giles on, 69
Preachers, Giles on, 53, 91
Prelates, negligence of, Giles on, 74
Protomartyrs of the Franciscan Order, 74

Q

Quaracchi editions of Franciscan works, x n, xv, xlii n, lx
Quattrosanti, Monastery of, xxiii
"Quellen zur Geschichte," etc. See Goetz
Questions, Notable, settled by Giles, 76

R

Recollection of death, Giles on, 67
Relics, Medieval rivalry to possess, xli
Religion and its safety, Giles on, 60
"Repertorium Biblicum," lvii n
Riche, Abbé, lviii n
Rieti, xxiv
Rivotorto, xvi, xvii
Rodolfo of Tossignano, lvi
Roland, Song of, 61 n
Rome, xxii
Rossi, Professor A., xliv n
Rufino, S. See Church
Rufinus, Brother, 30 n
Rule of the Friars Minor, date of its approbation by Innocent III, xv, quoted, 1
Ruskin on St. Louis's visit to Giles, xxxv

S

Sabatier, Paul, x, xi, xii n, xv, xvii, li n, liii n. See

also "Actus B. Francisci" and "Speculum Perfectionis"
Salamanca, lvi
Salimbene, Fra, chronicler, ix, xxvi n, xxxvi n, xlii
Salter, E. G. See "Franciscan Legends"
San Sesto, xxiv
Sayings of Blessed Brother Giles, their preëminence among early Franciscan ascetical works, vii; they reveal his genius and character more accurately than any legend or likeness, xlvi; their origin, xlvii; disclose the early Franciscan teaching, xlviii; high authority of, xlix; their characteristics and charm, l; their collection, li; date from thirteenth century, lii; for MSS. containing them see Manuscript Editions; translation of, see Translations appended to Fioretti, lvii; no trace of Douai translation which Sbaralea attributes to Fr. Angelus Mason, lix; need of a new English version, lx; opportune appearance of critical Latin edition at Quaracchi, lx; difficulties encountered by the editors in preparing the same, lx; their classification of MSS., xli; variants, lxi; difficulties of rendering original in English, lxii. For subject-matter of "Sayings," see Table of Contents
Sbaralea, J. H., lvi, lix
Schöffer, Peter, lv
Schoutens, Fr. Stephen, lix n
"Scriptores Ordinis Minorum," 2
Scripture, Sacred, quotations from: Exodus 25:4, 50; I Kings 3, 66; I Kings 16:7, 50; IV Kings 3:15, xxx; Ps. 16:15, 47; Ps. 26:4, 109; Ps. 30:20, 84; Ps. 33:9, 47, 84; Ps. 118:32, 55; Ps. 118:165, 84; Ps. 127:2, xxiv; Proverbs 3:32, 107; Proverbs 4:23, 103; Canticles 1:3, 46; Eccli. 20:8, 107; Isaias 58:7, 44; Jeremias 9:4, 9; Jeremias 15:19, 56; Malachias 3:6 52; Matthew 6:26, 29; Matthew 19:29, 45; Matthew 25:35, 44; Mark 10:30, 45; Luke 10:39, 47; Luke 10:41, 48; Luke 14:26, xxxix; Luke 17:10, 98, 113; Luke 22:32, 50; Luke 18:30, 45; Luke 19:13, 98; John 4:23, 44; John 4:24, 72; John 4:38, 98; I Tim. 5:6, 32; II Tim. 2:5, 114; Hebrews 1:12, 52; Hebrews 4:12, 3; I John 3:13, 53
Sedulius, H., lvi
Septem gradus Contemplationis, xlix
Shunning the world, Giles on, 68
Siena, xxvi n
Simon, Brother, 30 n

Solicitude, Giles on holy, 23
"Some Pages of Franciscan History," ix n
Spain, Giles's journey to, xx
"Speculum Monachorum," 107 n
"Speculum Perfectionis," ed. Sabatier, xvii, liii n, 11 n, 61 n
Spiritual caution, Giles on, 57
St. Damian's, xxviii
St. James of Compostella, Giles's pilgrimage to, xx
St. Joan d'Acre, xxi
"Storia Compendiosa." See Panfilo
"Storia d'Assisi." See Cristofani
"Storia di S. Francesco." See Papini
Suppression in Italy, xliii
Surius, L., lvi
Symonds, Margaret. See "Story of Perugia"

T

Thaddeus, O.F.M., Father, quoted, lix n
"Theologisch-praktische Quartalschrift," vii
Translations of the Golden Sayings: Dutch, lviii; English, lviii, lix, lxi, lxii; Flemish, lix; French, lviii; German, lviii; Italian, lvii
Trasimeno, xxi
Tunis, xxv
Tuscany, xxvi

U

Umbria, xxvi, xxxiii

V

Van Ortroy, S. J., Father, quoted, x n, xi, li n
Virtues acquired in prayer, Giles on, 71
Virtues and vices, Giles on, 4

W

Wadding, Luke, xv, xlii, lvi, 2. See also "Annales Minorum" and "Scriptores"
Watchfulness of heart, Giles on, 23
Words, Giles on good, 56
Working, Giles on, 91

Z

Zell, Ulr., lv

Milton Keynes UK
Ingram Content Group UK Ltd.
UKHW010308170224
437973UK00007B/709